THE EXPERT

WITNESS

IN YOU

Jeff Whitfield

The Expert Witness in You by Jeff Whitfield

∞

Amazon Kindle Electronic Book 2nd Edition 2022

∞

First published as an eBook in Great Britain in 2020

By FIDUS BOOKS,

an imprint of Fidus Press

∞

Books by this Author

Conflicts in Construction. Wiley Blackwell. 1994/2012.

Assessing Loss and Expense. RIBA Books. 1995/2013.

The Expert Witness in You. Fidus Press. 2022

The Ultimate Guide to The Best Orlando Holiday Ever! Fidus. 2022.

Authors Note: 2022 Edition

Dear Reader,

I do hope that you enjoy reading this book and learn from it. If you don't, just remember that it cost you less than a three topping pizza and you will surely feel better about things.

My life has been inextricably linked to building from being very young. I have always appreciated the effort and time that is expended in constructing our built environment. I have always loved building things myself. Even today, I often partner with my grandson to make intricate Lego models, albeit he would argue that mine is a more supervisory role.

Given my regard for a well planned and executed project, I recoiled a little when reading Neil de Grassi's book, *Astrophysics for People in a Hurry*, where he states that the universe was once one trillionth of the size of a full stop, then in a trillionth of a second the Big Bang had turned that invisible speck into the universe we now know and love. Now, I do love Neil, he is a great man, but I struggle with the theory that the cosmos went from almost nothing to a gigantic, organised life sustaining universe so rapidly when it took almost nine months to build our local Tesco.

Personally, I believe in the philosophy of Universal Grand Design, albeit when I see brutalist tower blocks from the 1960's I do wonder where the grand designer was when they were conceived. Perhaps he took a ten-year career break, only to return and regret leaving 'Concrete Joe' in charge.

When I was an errant child, I was told to always tell the truth. When I asked why I was simply told that it was expected. Life has taught me that the key reason for telling the truth is that you will become dependable. I soon realised that if you were caught in a lie you may never be trusted again, and what a burden that would be to carry through life. 'Nice chap but thoroughly unreliable', I was once told by a former cabinet minister who had just introduced me to a ministerial colleague.

If this book is taken to heart it should set you on the path to expert dependability, dependability being the key reason a qualified expert is selected.

I come from a family of expert witnesses. I have personally been giving expert testimony for 28 years, my oldest son is a Testifying Expert in Forensic Computing in the USA and he lectures around the World for SANS on his favoured topic. My third son has been a Testifying expert for almost ten years and is a Cyber Crime specialist with a UK Police Force. He gives expert testimony on those unpleasant and unsettling criminal matters where computers and mobile phones have been forensically examined and evidence, often photographic, extracted.

The advice given herein is largely personal, based on our varied experiences, and is often anecdotal. Given time you will develop your own expert style and you will soon have your own stories to tell.

Follow the basic principles I have outlined, and you will ably assist Tribunals and serve your clients well.

Jeff Whitfield.

November 2022

Preface.

When I wrote the first of my seven articles on how to be an expert witness over a decade ago, I had no idea how much correspondence and interest it would generate.

In the next year I wrote six more articles and produced seven podcasts whilst working with Hill International. To be honest, I had noticed that JK Rowling had produced seven books in her Harry Potter series and as a result had sold millions. Sadly, my clever ploy failed; the rule of seven let me down, and I enjoyed just a few thousand downloads. So, unlike JK Rowling, I didn't need an army of personal assistants to answer my email.

Some of you will already know that under a pseudonym I have written thriller novels for over a decade. Before that I wrote two construction books related to disputes. In my experience, when construction authors' books sell over ten thousand copies, we tend to celebrate with a champagne party and dance the night away with the Kardashians. In contrast, when my novels hit the 1.5 million sales/downloads I called my publisher, who simply pointed out that Agatha Christie had written seventy novels by the time she was my age.

This imbalance in sales expectation between learned texts and novels reminded me of a story my comic/musician father used to tell about a church organist who moonlighted in a local social club. When asked how much he earned as a church organist the man replied, "A few hundred pounds a year." When asked the same question about his moonlighting job, he grinned and replied, "Ten thousand pounds last year." "How do feel about that?" the reporter asked. The organist didn't answer but instead turned to the old pipe organ in the empty church and belted out a familiar tune whilst singing at the top of his voice, "There's no business, like showbusiness!"

Fiction sells, but factual books help to change attitudes and improve lives.

Enjoy this book. It took my whole career to research - but pardon me if I break out into song at my desk.

"There's no business, like show business...."

Contents:

Section 1:

What Constitutes an Expert Witness in the 2020's?

1.1 Expert Beginnings

As I grew up, I was always curious about the things going on around me and I marvelled at the inefficient ways in which things were done. As a result, when I was assigned dull household chores, I sought out efficient ways of doing my work, largely so that I could get back to my books or my football.

My newspaper delivery round became a work of art. After a year on the same route there was never a step wasted. At weekends I worked on a farm and I developed a new strategy for harvesting the field of turnips. I was paid nine shillings (45p) for each row of turnips, and the farmer expected two rows a day to be turned up by the tractor and then topped and tailed by the farmhand before being placed on the tractor flatbed. By the time I finished harvesting, I was completing four rows a day and using the tractor much less than the adult farm hands. I was fourteen at the time and £1.80 for a day's work was more than I earned all week delivering morning and evening papers.

When I left my job at the farm, I drew the farmer a diagram of how I achieved my four rows of turnips per day and the farmer was glowing in his praise. He sent my mother free turnips every year after that until she moved away. I enjoyed the feeling of being an expert in something, and soon I was hooked on giving people advice.

I was obliged to pay my own way through building college, as neither of my parents was contributing to my upkeep. At the age of sixteen they suspected I had more money in the bank than they did, and they were right. So, I took a job in a cobbler's shop. I was a counter assistant, and I also did the simpler repairs. When passing trade failed to deliver enough repair orders, I suggested that I go out and canvass for shoes that needed repair. I received a commission or every new order and was soon making more than my cobbler's salary. My strategy? I targeted the local flats. There were three blocks local to me, each block housed 100 flats and it was only five yards from door to door. The corridors were all inside and so I never got wet when it rained. Being honest, I really enjoyed replacing soles and heels and repairing shoes generally. It was a largely therapeutic expertise that is all but lost in this modern age. Many years later, I discovered from my uncle that my grandfather had been a part time shoe repairer between the wars, supplementing his meagre income as a council foreman.

In the 1970's, when I began full time work as a trainee quantity surveyor, I soon recognised that the older staff hated coding their measurements for the purpose of creating computer aided production of bills of quantities (BoQ's). Having identified this niche in the market, I specialised in the collation, coding and computerisation of the measured works, so that the luddite QS's could concentrate on taking-off in the manner they always had. To be fair, the original luddites ran amok, destroying any modern machinery in their domain, but my older, conservatively minded QS colleagues drew a line at such behaviour.

So it was that at a youthful eighteen years old I found myself liaising with UK experts in the computer production of BoQ's, Specifications and the co-ordination of computer language to suit the Standard Method of Measurement. At the age of 23 - I looked older, I suspect - I was nominated by the local authorities' representative body to work on the consultative committees for SMM6 and SMM7.

So, by my early twenties I had already discovered, albeit inadvertently, that not only did I enjoy being an expert (of sorts) but that it led to recognition, faster promotion and better pay.

I recount this brief history because I want you to understand that you are all experts in your own speciality. What you need to do is hone your existing skills, watch for opportunities, and be bold enough to specialise.

By the end of this book, I intend to uncover the expert witness in you.

1.2 Defining the Expert Role.

As a professional who has acted as an expert witness for over 28 years, I would like to say that expert witnesses enjoy the luxury of being an exceedingly rare and very highly qualified, or experienced, commodity. Sadly, this simply is not so.

The fact of the matter is that tribunals all over the world, in all of their multi-faceted forms, commonly rely on expert opinion because their own experience in very technical matters can be close to non-existent. There are many thousands of actions every year and as many as ten experts in an action. Experts are not a species on the endangered list.

One of my favoured definitions of an expert witness, as instructed in legal proceedings, is as follows: "An expert witness is a person who, by virtue of education, training, certification, skills or experience, is accepted by a judge or tribunal as an expert in their field."

If these experts have the necessary experience and qualifications, a judge or tribunal may consider an expert witness's specialised (scientific, technical or other) opinion about evidence, or about facts, to be an "expert opinion". But only insofar as the expert has not strayed from their area of particular expertise.

As you would expect in any adversarial dispute resolution system, expert opinions and testimony will be challenged under cross examination, and they can be rebutted by testimony from other experts or by the presentation of other evidence or facts.

1.3 Historical Background

Wikipedia helpfully explains that forensic expert practice is an ancient profession. It notes that in ancient Babylonia, midwives were used as experts in determining pregnancy, virginity and female fertility. Similarly, the Roman Empire recognized midwives, handwriting experts and land surveyors as legal experts.

In my legal studies I discovered that Architects and Quantity Surveyors had been called as expert witnesses for almost two centuries and have, consequently, been quoted widely in some landmark contract law cases from the Victorian era onwards.

The accepted definition of what duties an expert witness should fulfil, serve to remind us that the codified use of expert witnesses and the admissibility of their testimony and scientific evidence has developed significantly in the courts in the last 250 years. The use of expert witnesses will, no doubt, continue to increase as the world becomes more complex and more automated.

The research I carried out for this book led me to agree with a friend and dedicated university lecturer, who always commenced her courses on expert witness work by citing academic texts that she summarised as follows:

"Generally speaking, the concept of allowing an expert witness to testify in a court setting, and provide opinionated evidence on the facts of other witnesses, was first introduced by Lord Mansfield in the case of Folkes v. Chadd (1872) Douglas' King's Bench Reports (3) p157.'

In that particular case, the court was hearing litigation relating to the silting of Wells Harbour in Norfolk and the court allowed leading civil engineer, John Smeaton, to provide opinion evidence. This decision by the English Courts to allow Mr Smeaton to provide necessary contextual background and detail on a case is often cited by historians as being at the root of modern rules on expert testimony."

1.4 The Use of Experts.

As I have noted above, judges are generally exceptional lawyers who need professionals such as Architects, Doctors, Engineers and Surveyors to guide them through the intricacies of a profession, trade or occupation quite different from their own.

Having cited my own definition of judges, I note that real life experiences have placed me in front of judges who were as capable of understanding accounts as the best forensic accountant and judges whose understanding of forensic medical evidence almost precluded the need for additional expertise.

There have also been some notable engineers and construction professionals who channelled their skills into the law, as barristers, and who then became judges later in their career. These exemplary judges may have had less need for expert guidance, but they still allow them to be called. Nevertheless, in the main, Judges are fine lawyers who need your help.

At this point some readers may be querying my use of the expression 'profession, trades or occupation' in my opening sentence in this sub section. I make no excuse for my inclusion of 'trades and occupations' in the expert category. There is no reason at all why a proficient tradesman should not be called to be an expert witness. Likewise, a talented administrator may really help the court in understanding complex or intricate office procedures.

In the late 1990's, I was involved as an expert witness in a construction case where the welding on a major new bridge was an issue. The plaintiff controversially chose to rely upon their working welding foreman to explain the case for additional welding time and money. The defendant responded with evidence from an expert from a welding institute. The Judge, and I think all of those in attendance, knew immediately that the 'expert' welder had not welded a joint for decades. His evidence was largely theoretical, and data driven, whilst the foreman welder's evidence was less eloquent, but it was informed, relevant and gritty. Notwithstanding any deficiency in delivery, the welder's evidence was clearly heartfelt and, ultimately, persuasive.

If you have a trade skill, a talent or an interest that involves you in becoming proficient beyond the norm, you too could be an expert.

When I was a young surveyor, I worked with a trainee QS called Gary, who was likeable if a little odd. His great talent was playing a tune on his teeth, along with tapping his head (mouth opening and closing) to produce a vague hollow recognisable tune. My other colleagues believed that this *talent* was so universal that they could all replicate it with ease. However, despite their continual rehearsals (often misunderstood by 'passer's by' who gave them a wide berth for years afterwards) they found that they could not mimic his achievement. Eventually Gary's 15 minutes of fame arrived, and he appeared on That's Life, a quirky TV series from the 1970's and 1980's.

My answer to the question "Who can be an expert witness?" must therefore be anyone who has a special skill or expertise that can only be adequately described to a layman by a proponent of that skill.

1.5 The Range of Experts

The reason that experts vary so widely in discipline and background is largely due to the fact that the types of tribunals who seek their expert assistance also vary widely.

Tribunals will often be legally constituted bodies such as; a Judge or Judges sitting in a variety of Law Courts, a single arbitrator or panel of arbitrators sitting in Arbitration hearings, adjudicators sitting alone under some legislative enactment or, individuals nominated to sit on employment tribunals of all types. Occasionally regulatory tribunals will be bodies comprised of non-legal professionals sitting in judgement of a fellow professional. Let me give you a few obvious examples of how and when experts may be needed.

When deciding whether to compensate a contractor whose project was massively delayed and whose profits were washed away by the summer rain, a tribunal might need to know how often it normally rains in July in Prestatyn. In such a case the Meteorological office could probably supply an appropriate expert and supporting data.

The Civil Aviation Authorities may wish to advise airlines just how much volcanic ash is "too much" for aircraft to pass through safely, while engineers and volcanic ash scientists should have the expertise to be able to assist.

When does a virus spread so widely that it becomes a pandemic, and what can be done to manage the pandemic? Doctors, statisticians, and population analysts can be called upon to offer expert opinions.

A project finishes late and over budget, so where should the losses lie? Programming and Quantum experts can be instructed to analyse the events and discover the causes of such overruns.

1.6 A Tribunal's Task

Tribunals are usually tasked with choosing between several reasonable sounding options. In such cases they are trying to decide which option is closer to being right and which is closer to being wrong, and whether too much uncertainty remains. Essentially, tribunals want to know what can be done to provide the most equitable outcome, in accordance with the law.

As such, as an expert you could reasonably be expected to receive instructions in a variety of circumstances, including:

1) Disputed Liability. In a negligence case you may be asked to opine on whether the defendant, perhaps a fellow professional, exercised the appropriate duty of care in executing their work or their design. If they did not, then they may be liable to repay damages.

2) Disputed Damages. Once a party has been found liable the tribunal may want to know how much time or money should be allowed. You may be able to calculate the damage for the tribunal.

3) Lack of understanding. Your task may be simply to advise or assist the tribunal in comprehending a complex technical issue, explaining it in layman's terms so that the tribunal can gauge the implications of any failure.

4) Research. The Tribunal may need new data that does not currently exist, or you may be tasked with providing updated data where the available information may be unreliable or out of date.

5) Analysis. You may be asked to give your opinion on a person, their behaviour, or their actions to assist a tribunal in knowing how to apply an appropriate sentence or how best to manage their future treatment or recovery.

There are, no doubt, many more circumstances where your expertise and mine can be utilised, and we need to seek them out.

I have been instructed mostly on civil cases but have opined on three criminal cases, too. We must never underestimate how useful our knowledge, experience and qualifications can be. This section is designed to give you a bare understanding of the scope of expert work. As the future unfolds, new opportunities will arise for those ready for a challenge.

1.6 Recognising a Reliable Expert Witness

As noted above, an Expert Witness is an individual who has useful expertise and/or experience beyond that of the man in the street, and whose genuine opinion can assist a tribunal in finding a solution to problem they face. But can we identify explicit expert behaviours that will help us to identify a credible expert?

Luckily, life hands us the gift of experience and we will continually learn more about ourselves, and others, as time passes. That accrued life knowledge enables us to grow in both wisdom and learning. These experiences do not always come from the expected places.

Some years ago, I was pressed (by family members) to participate in a TV quiz programme on the BBC. In all honesty, appearing on the *Weakest Link* was quite nerve wracking. Not because of the redoubtable Anne Robinson, but because I did not wish to appear stupid to a national TV audience. I was also determined not to make the "walk of shame" at the end of round one, only to see a professional dog walker from Purley go on to win the cash.

I didn't win, and I don't expect you to believe this, but I actually knew the answers to everyone else's questions.

So, did I learn anything from a day at Pinewood Studios? Did my moment of TV fame make any impact on the way I approach expert assignments? In a way, it did. I learned some valuable lessons during filming that are pertinent to experts everywhere, and which I will not forget quickly, such as:

- Don't submit yourself for questioning unless you know the topic.
- Don't guess the answer; it is probably going to be wrong.
- Don't shrivel under the withering gaze of a dominant questioner, answer quickly, boldly and with conviction.

Observing these basic three principles will ensure that your hard-earned reputation as an expert witness remains untarnished, so perhaps we should examine each trait in turn.

An Expert should always know their topic

As an expert witness in the built environment, a good quantum expert is expected to have an abundant knowledge of construction methods and the measurement thereof. The expert will understand the original contracted scope of work, the site application of the materials in use and quantities required to fulfil that scope. Finally, they will know how the contract deals with the measurement and evaluation of changes to the works.

Likewise, a programming expert will not only know how to manipulate planning software but will be experienced in constructional methods and will be practical in their application. The expert will not only understand the processes of construction but will know how long an activity should take. The forensic programming expert will also know how the works *should* have been logically sequenced. Armed with this knowledge, they can provide a tribunal with a fact-based analysis and a worthy opinion.

A medical expert witness will usually be professionally qualified, well trained and will probably continue to practice at the highest level of his profession. Medical advances are so frequent and so dramatic that a practitioner who has been away from practice, or who has solely concentrated on forensic expert work, even for a couple of years, may not be a reliable expert witness on matters of current practice.

It all sounds so obvious when it is written down in a book, and whilst it is quite a simple set of rules, there are still many Expert Witnesses who fail to meet even the basic criteria set out above.

For example, a year ago I was called in to assess an engineering project in London which seriously overran the programmed completion date. The Contractors' Programming Expert Witness accepted that the Contractor's extension of time claim was valid, even though it sought an extension of time on the basis of an expert analysis that forecast a *planned* completion date months beyond the *actual* completion date.

Disregarding strenuous arguments from me in expert discussions, and later from the tribunal in the hearing, each of us pointing out the obvious flaws in such an expert finding, the expert remained firm. Then, despite being referred to earlier cases and learned academic texts to the contrary by counsel, the expert remained immovable. Inevitably, during cross examination, the expert faced the accusation that his findings were wholly "theoretical" and that as a matter of record the events did not happen at the times shown on his theoretical analysis. Despite all of the advice, the Expert refused to move from his stated position and a chance to narrow the issues was lost, as was his client's case.

Experts must not guess

The Chancellor to Henry VIII, Cardinal Wolsey, once said *"A man may believe what he will, but he should believe what he ought"*. In my view experts are allowed to have an opinion, but that opinion must not disregard the evidence. An Expert's opinion should only be constructed under the strict criteria befitting the independence of the role, namely:

1. It should be on a matter upon which they are informed.
2. It should be on a matter upon which they are experienced.
3. It should be on a matter upon which they are qualified to opine.
4. It should always be based upon known facts, where these are available.
5. If contemporaneous facts are not available, any published data relied upon must be from a reputable and reliable source.
6. Where it is a best estimate or guess, this should be clearly noted.

In an arbitration on an overseas power project in 2010, the Contractor's expert (an engineer) was unable to verify the price of the Contractor's bulk materials. Rather than carry out a measure of installed works (as per the contract) the expert assumed that the total weights of pipeline materials delivered had been installed. He then applied an estimating rate and labour norms to the total delivered weights and valued the work accordingly.

Under detailed cross examination it was disclosed that the Contractor's expert had not been able to find accurate weights for the numerous different valves delivered, and so he had allocated them into columns of "less than 2kg", "2kg to 10kg" and "10kg to 20kg", whilst making the assumption that every valve in each column was equal to the maximum weight in the column heading i.e. 2kg, 10kg and 20kg respectively. This guess proved to be completely wrong, with the cost of many valves being as little as 30% of that weight allowed by the expert. Additionally, the exercise was flawed because the expert had allowed the labour for fixing all of the delivered pipework, disregarding the fact that around 5% to 10% of the delivered pipework would typically be discarded as wastage.

This use of guesswork was wholly avoidable as the necessary valve weight information was available on the internet, just a few mouse clicks away, and the installed pipework was still visible and could be measured on site or from record drawings.

Guessing simply is not acceptable behaviour for an expert, and if experts are asked to give an educated or informed guess then they should make it clear that their answer is an approximation based on their experience. Only poor experts make assumptions, where real evidence can be uncovered.

Experts should be sure of their opinions

This heading might also be entitled; Experts should research their own work and reach their own opinions. Again, whilst this appears to be an obvious point, many experts do not comply with this basic rule and will take on more cases that they can possibly handle. This means they must pass on much of the work of opinion forming onto less experienced staff. This is extremely dangerous, and it is the very antithesis of the reason why the courts allow genuine experts to testify.

When an expert has carried out their own research thoroughly, has found sound evidence upon which to rely, and has then formulated an honestly held opinion based on experience, they are better placed than anyone else to influence the tribunal.

Advocates, no matter how skilled and informed, cannot (or should not) know the Expert's turf better than the expert, yet they sometimes manage to persuade experts that they do. If the Expert has prepared their own work properly, they should know where to find the answers to all relevant and important questions. Where the bulk of the difficult questions have been answered firmly and with precision, an expert can safely confess to the tribunal that they do not know the answer to certain questions. There is no shame in not being omniscient, nor is it expected.

Perhaps because of nerves, or maybe due to lack of preparation, experts can occasionally be knocked off course by aggressive questioning. If you are, or are hoping to become, an expert, you must remember that forming an opinion is only a small part of the expert's job. Defending your opinion in the face of hostile cross examination is potentially the more important part.

To share an example of exactly what I mean I refer to a recent case. A short while ago I watched as experienced counsel took an expert to task on their report. The expert clearly had not done their own research and soon became nervous as they realised that some of their reported opinions were not sustainable, given the facts. Counsel smelled blood and moved up a gear. The expert stammered and shook. At one point the expert conceded that much of the work had been done by others. Very soon their opinion was destroyed. Later, when the expert had the transcripts read out to them, they were stunned. They had no recollection of accepting the premise that the opposing expert's view was probably more prescient than their own.

Facing experienced counsel in cross examination is difficult and may even border on traumatic, but the expert should remember that on the issues in question, they should always be better informed about their own report than opposing counsel.

In my experience, firm, bold answers drawn from the documents will help to unsettle the cross examiner, who is always anxious to avoid reinforcing the opposing expert's unwanted opinion.

Understandably, for clients, choosing a reliable expert can be tricky. Will the expert do the research? Can they trust the expert not to guess? Will the expert fold under hostile questioning? Only time will tell, unless the legal team chooses wisely from the ranks of responsible experts, like you and I, who have been there, done the research, and many of whom have faced the rigours of testifying.

In this section we looked at a series of general definitions describing the role and persona of an expert witness. We also came to understand that there are expert witnesses to be found in many varied disciplines. Finally, we identified what good and bad behaviours are commonly displayed by experts in real life situations.

Next, we should examine the essential qualities demanded in a testifying expert witness - honesty, impartiality, independence, and integrity.

Section 2:

Honesty, Impartiality, Independence & Integrity

2.1 Referees

Over the years the judiciary has been mocked by the media. US cult TV series, such as Ally McBeal and Boston Legal, often poked fun at judges. In the UK, tabloid newspapers have targeted judges for personal humiliation when they claimed to be unaware of current celebrities or were found to be unfamiliar with contemporary technology. We have all seen the headlines suggesting that judges were too old or out of touch with modern society. That has never been my experience either in court or in front of tribunals.

Despite any negativity that we may see in the way judges are portrayed on UK TV programmes such as Silks and Law & Order UK, most judges, arbitrators, and adjudicators are very astute. I have seldom seen a well-read jurist make an outlandish award unless he or she was bound by the existing law to do so.

Oft times the least understandable decisions, for which judges are mercilessly mocked in the press, are forced upon them by precedent, legislation or by the poor pleading of one or other of the parties to a dispute.

2.2 Fairness and Equanimity

Tribunals of all kinds can be presumed to be calm, thoughtful, and independent. That is, they are generally unmoved by emotional outbursts and they make every effort to remain unbiased with regard to the parties before them. Being non prejudicial is difficult for human beings generally, and when we are obliged by our oaths to be so, it can be stressful.

Imagine a judge in a criminal case having to deal with a serial killer who has allegedly preyed on innocent children. Imagine that the killer enters the court with a smirk on their face and a not guilty plea on their lips.

Now imagine how difficult it must be for a decent judge with children or grandchildren of their own, to maintain his or her impartial role.

Our expert cases are unlikely to be so emotive, but we still encounter individuals and companies who appear to be amoral or even callous, and yet we still have a duty to ensure that *everyone* receives a fair hearing.

In this regard, it has been my experience that most individuals with a long history of standing in the role of impartial referee between two warring parties can listen to witnesses and determine their trustworthiness. In several cases I have heard words like these: "I preferred the evidence of Mr Smith to that of Mr Brown" uttered in judgements. I suspect that this is Judicial code for, "In my view Mr Brown was not being entirely truthful."

In one uncomfortable case I watched as my opposing expert sank lower and lower into his seat, as the Judge dismissed his expert report as being biased and reflected that the expert's opinion was that of a hired gun. The Judge went on to ask counsel how it was that this man could have been considered as an independent expert witness. He never was again.

So the question we are addressing here is really, how can we ensure that independence, impartiality, honesty and integrity continue to be the central pillars supporting our opinions?

As the best experts always do, we must continually examine ourselves and our work to ensure that we are following the rules, but how do we ensure that others are equally diligent in this regard? We will discuss that in a short while, but first let us look at the fundamentals as they relate to us.

2.3 Honesty

George Washington is often credited with being a sterling example of honesty. His biographer, Mason Locke Weems, illustrated the young George's honesty by way of an anecdote. He asserted that in his youth George cut down a favoured cherry tree in his father's garden and when his enraged father demanded that the culprit be identified, George stepped forward and said; "It was I, father, I cannot tell a lie!"

Historians now believe that this story only existed in the mind of the biographer, as it has no provenance in fact. Nonetheless, it is still used as a trope today. True or false, the expert lesson to be derived from this story is simply this; George Washington could not tell a lie, and nor should we.

Honesty is not flexible, and yet we are constantly bombarded with sayings that suggest it is. Many of these quotes come from the political arena. Here are some examples. What do you think of when you hear these statements?

- I was not lying; I was being economical with the truth.
- This isn't lying, it is political spin.
- You may think that, but I couldn't possibly comment.
- It is vital that our leaders have plausible deniability.
- They can have missiles over our military bases in 45 minutes.
- OK. You caught me in a lie, from now on I'll be truthful!

As an expert, if we know something is true, we may state it and use it as the basis of an opinion or finding. If we only suspect that it is true, we should make that distinction clear in our testimony.

Misleading people is also dishonesty. Let me give you an everyday example of a lie shrouded in misleading misinformation. A few years ago, I was on a strict diet and my wife quizzed me on my choice of lunchtime repast.

"What did you have for lunch?"

"Lettuce, tomato etc."

"A salad?"

"Oh, you know, lettuce tomato, onions, dressing, that kind of thing."

"What else did you have with these salad ingredients? were they perchance sandwiched in a bun with a burger and served with fries?"

I was burned. She knows me too well. But avoiding giving an honest answer when you know the answer is dishonest, despite philosophical arguments to the contrary.

Honesty is not only central to our expert role; it is vital if we are to protect our stellar reputation. Once you have been caught lying to or misleading someone it will be difficult to change their perception of you as a deceiver in the future.

2.4 Discerning Honesty and Integrity in Others.

Discernment is a much under used faculty that is one of the free gifts bestowed on mankind. Part instinct, part experiential learning, it also encompasses spiritual elements, according to some. Over the centuries, philosophers, from Socrates and Plato to Bertrand Russell and Jean-Paul Sartre, have acknowledged that on occasion, individuals appear to have foreknowledge of things they have no right to know. Sometimes it is ascribed to mysticism or religion. Mostly it is just as puzzling to the ingenious as it is to the ignorant.

Notwithstanding our lack of understanding as to its source, we should be happy to benefit from the presence of discernment in our daily life.

So, what does discernment look like in everyday life?

Have you ever hesitated before doing something, only to find that your hesitation saved you from injury or harm? Well, these feelings, whilst not one hundred percent reliable, should not be ignored. If something feels wrong to you, trust your instinct and investigate further. Great experts listen to that still small voice and are sometimes better off for it.

As a youth in Yorkshire I recall being introduced to a man who had been presented to me as a successful DJ, friend to the poor and tireless charity worker. He was admired by all, and yet I shuddered when we shook hands. I kept my distance from that day on, concerned that I had such negative feelings for a man with no grounds whatsoever. That man was Jimmy Savile. Our instincts are designed to save us from harm. Rely upon them.

If you prefer to utilise more prosaic methods of discerning the truth, here are some practical guidelines. As with most guidelines these are not infallible. On occasion you will find a liar convincing and an honest man quite unbelievable. You may also come across an expert who is sincerely convinced of the correctness of their own case despite an avalanche of evidence to the contrary.

Remember Cardinal Wolsey's quote from earlier in the text: "A man can believe what he will, but he should believe what he ought." This concept brings me to my first personal expert rule on discerning honesty and intent in others.

If an expert offers an opinion that relies neither on stated fact, nor on his training or experience, then he ought not to be offering that opinion in front of a tribunal of any kind.

I have been described by my friends as a kind of benign egotist, one who holds a firm, sometimes controversial, opinion on many issues. I am, however, properly qualified to offer an opinion to a tribunal on very few issues.

For example, I may believe that a flat rate of income tax starting at progressive levels - dependent upon an individual's circumstances - would be simple, fair and inexpensive to administer. I may say that I would allow no avoidance, no allowances and no excuses. You earn/ receive more that £40,000.00 in a year you pay 25% tax on everything above that figure. I may have that opinion, but I am not in possession of the figures showing who would be affected by my system of taxation and how. Neither do I know whether this system would collect enough tax or too much tax. That opinion would be based on an incomplete knowledge and it may well have to change when I have been apprised of the true facts. I am perfectly entitled to offer my opinion as a proposition, but I cannot offer it as expert evidence, because I am inexpert in general taxation.

So, to my rule number two:

If an expert confronted with contradictory evidence refuses to change their opinion, we are quite properly entitled to assume that they are biased in favour of their client and that they may not be expressing a genuine or honest opinion.

A well-known Victorian statesman and parliamentarian once exclaimed, "Sir, you may change my mind, but you will not change my vote". Evidence of such blind loyalty in an opposing expert should alert us to the potential for a less than genuine opinion to be published.

We should test an expert's opinion (or honesty) by asking probing questions.

My third rule, above, provides another way we can find the truth of things, and it is by far the most popular method. It is a method well known to us all. It has enabled parents to see through childish lies with relative ease for generations past. That method is questioning. In court we call it cross examination, but it works equally well in everyday life without any oath being sworn. Imagine this conversation:

Parent to a six-year-old child: You are late. Where have you been?

Child: I would have been on time, but there was a Martian at the end of the street, and I had to hide until he had gone.

Parent: Really? That must have been exciting. How tall was he?

Child: About your height!

Parent: That's odd. Martians are usually as tall as a house!

Child: He was, I just remembered, he was as tall as a house......

As a parent to four children I have had many such conversations, even when they were in their twenties. They were a little more accomplished at lying by then, of course, but not quite good enough.

If you don't know enough about a subject to ask sensible questions, carry out your own research.

My fourth, and final, expert rule in this arena, suggests another way of discerning honesty, which is, do your own research. If someone offers you an opinion you can often check the legitimacy of their base evidence very quickly. At one time this meant much research in libraries, encyclopaedias, and the time-consuming task of seeking out experts. Today we have mobile phones armed with Bing, Google, and Ask Jeeves, which can be used as our primary sources of enquiry.

It is now possible to find out very quickly, via the internet, what alternative opinions and views are available for us to consider. We may even uncover irrefutable evidence that the opinion we were offered is wrong.

Two years ago, I was in a court when a witness explained a technical term incorrectly. The majority of the court appeared none the wiser, but the Judge was immediately suspicious. From a laptop on the bench the judge *googled* the term and found the real meaning. The judge then interrupted the witness and offered the witness the opportunity to reconsider their definition. The witness acknowledged the error but remained shaky for the rest of their testimony.

So, in summary:

Rule 1: Challenge opinion evidence from an individual who lacks the training, experience, or knowledge to offer such an opinion.

Rule 2: If the evidence changes and the opinion should also change but does not, do not accept the expert's impartiality at face value.

Rule 3: Always test opinions by asking questions.

Rule 4: You may need to research the subject yourself to be able to ask searching questions or to find alternative views to put to the expert.

2.5 Maintaining Honesty and Integrity in Ourselves.

We should now understand how to identify a less than honest opinion from others, but how do we ensure that we *remain* independent and unbiased ourselves? I am going to suggest that a cursory understanding of psychology could help.

Pop Psychology

When instructed by clients to assist in resolving a dispute you may be perplexed by the attitude of the opposing experts, who seem to be in a state of denial about the *obvious* facts. It might appear, therefore, that the opposition are either naive or are lying.

Whilst in some situations individuals do lie to protect themselves or others, it may be also be the case that their behaviour results from a less cynical human behaviour, an unconscious psychological process. Two particular psychological processes that could be to blame are:

- Cognitive dissonance, and,
- Confirmative bias

You might ask why as expert witnesses we should concern ourselves with quasi psychological issues. The answer is that as expert witnesses we deal as much with people as we do with facts.

In the 1990's I wrote a book, Conflicts in Construction, which dealt with both the psychological and anthropological issues present in construction conflicts, and since then I have kept an open dialogue with practitioners in both business psychology and business anthropology. I would like you to benefit from the valuable insights shared with me by professors in both disciplines over the years. I would also like you to buy the Second Edition originally published in 2011 by Wiley-Blackwell, but that is your decision.

Whether or not you read more widely on the topic, there is wisdom in understanding normal interpersonal human relationships in an industry where we deal with people as much as we do with things.

Dealing with Internal Conflict

During my years of observing expert witnesses involved in the resolution of disputes, it has become clear to me that, in common with human beings generally, experts do not cope well with unresolved internal conflict.

A common example of an internal conflict might be the decision to buy a house. We study the market but, inevitably, the market does not offer us the ideal house at the ideal price, and so we compromise, often choosing between two less than ideal options. This leaves us conflicted because we are constantly asking the questions; would I have found my ideal house if I had waited? Have I acted too quickly?

Add to this the unsettling fact that the house chosen seems to have defects or disadvantages (that other choices may not have had) and we begin to feel uncomfortable with our decision, and we may even suffer from "buyer's remorse".

Self-aware, well-educated, and highly qualified Expert Witnesses often cope poorly with the thought that they may have made a mistake, even though they understand that intricate professional decisions carry risks. As Expert Witnesses we must be ready to accept new information or data and factor it into our opinions, however unsettling that may be for us and the client. An expert's fully informed and honest opinion is the proper opinion.

Whilst we can understand that it may be difficult for individuals with a certain self-image to live with the possibility that they may have acted imperfectly, we should recognise that it is often because they find it hard to forgive themselves for perceived errors.

The truth is that for most human beings dwelling on their errors creates unhappiness and dysfunction. To manage this situation, the human brain has developed two automatic defensive mechanisms which enable us to manage these feelings of despair and regain full functionality. They are the aforementioned,

- Cognitive dissonance, and,
- Confirmative bias

We will deal with cognitive dissonance first.

2.6 Cognitive Dissonance

The theory of cognitive dissonance states that; *contradicting cognitions serve as a driving force that compels the mind to acquire or invent new thoughts or beliefs, or to modify existing beliefs, so as to reduce the amount of dissonance (conflict) between cognitions.*

Human beings in general, and even level minded experts, are not immune to this behaviour. People are apt to invent or accept alternative theories supporting their original opinion, rather than accept that their initial views were wrongly held.

In the middle of the last century a sect grew up around a prophecy that aliens would destroy the world in the mid 1950's. When the world was not destroyed as prophesied, the cult members were conflicted. They still believed in their prophet, but his prophecy was clearly wrong. They could not live in harmony in the face of this conflict for long, and so when a different prophetess spoke out in 1957 explaining that the aliens had spared the planet for their sakes, they accepted this reasoning with enthusiasm. In short, they now had a reason to go on believing as they always had.

This type of behaviour exists, in a less extreme form, in the dispute resolution process. A claimant will allege a cause of loss, and will champion that cause of loss with vigour, without thoroughly investigating the true cause of the loss. Then, when the facts are researched and it appears that the alleged cause was not, as a matter of fact, the actual cause of the loss, the claimant becomes conflicted. Psychologically, the claimant wants to believe that their original assertion is correct, but the facts suggest otherwise. Luckily for the claimant, a consultant happens along who is able to produce a report which supports the claimant's original allegations - thus removing the conflict. The claimant can now happily believe they are in the right once again.

2.7 Confirmative Bias

A similar process occurs with the more common human behaviour of confirmative bias. The term confirmative bias refers to an aspect of human behaviour which induces us to reinforce our existing beliefs, often at the expense of *all* of the facts. To refer back to the example of the choice between two houses mentioned earlier, this might work as follows.

We move into the house we have chosen and find that the property tax is lower than we initially thought, and we save £120 per year. This confirms to us our wise decision to buy this particular house, and so we congratulate ourselves. Later we discover that the house is situated in an area which allegedly has a higher risk of burglary, and our insurance premium rises by £240 per year. We attribute our overall loss to those greedy, grasping insurers who are anxious to make a profit from our custom. Thus vindicating our original, clever decision.

Some psychologists will argue that as human beings we are instinctively (perhaps unconsciously) inclined to seek evidence that will support our existing beliefs, but when we are acting as expert witnesses, we cannot take that untroubled path. All expert witnesses must be true to the facts and so we must examine *all* available data before forming an objective opinion.

In construction disputes we see confirmative bias regularly from both claimants and their consultants. We can even find examples in expert witness reports and expert testimony. In the construction dispute setting, an example of confirmative bias may work as follows:

a) The client makes an assertion as to why, in their opinion, the roof was late completing.
b) The claims consultant seeks confirmation that the roof was late for the stated reason, *confining any research to those documents supporting the client's assertion.*
c) Naturally the research supports the assertion and so reinforces the belief in the client's case.

Confirmative bias is a natural human behaviour that is often calming and quite harmless, but it ceases to be harmless when this behaviour migrates into the expert witness arena where huge dispute costs can be incurred because one or both parties rely upon poorly researched opinions.

As you can imagine, confirmative bias can become truly devastating if it migrates into a geopolitical setting such as: "The decision to go to war is right because….".

In some extreme cases, if confirmative bias is to offer any real comfort, individuals will be obliged to *actively* avoid coming into contact with the truth.

In a radio interview with a controversial former presidential press secretary it was noted that the US Presidential press spokesman is often excluded from important decision-making meetings so that he or she cannot inadvertently disclose the true facts under pressure from the media. This is a cynical extension of the dubious concept the Americans have called "plausible deniability". Unfortunately, it also appears elsewhere in the world in construction disputes. To follow the example at a) to c) above, let us imagine that the claims consultant is still convinced that his client's case is supportable but:

- In two party meetings the consultant becomes aware of facts that support an alternative *theory* as to why the roof was late, but he chooses to ignore it because it emanates from an opposition source who could be perceived as being biased.

- The consultant is instructed not to pursue research into the alternative theory (or the consultant chooses not to do so) as there is a possibility that he may undermine his client's case (and his own earlier advice) by uncovering evidence that the client's assertion was misdirected.

This approach of applying selective evidence to a case is commonly adopted by claimants and their consultants but, more worryingly, it has also been used by expert witnesses. It is worth noting that expert witnesses caught operating in this manner have been harshly criticised by the courts and tribunals.

In short, like the US Presidential press spokesman cited above, a client with a tenuous case may hope to avoid the accusation of deliberate deceit by circumnavigating the truth and sustaining a comfortable ignorance. It simply won't work in a construction dispute that runs to a hearing, at least not for long.

In a court hearing a year or so ago an opposing expert witness had the opportunity to examine their own client's disclosed documentation but failed to do so. As a result, they were able to assert before the court, with a clear conscience, that a generalised claim was necessary because the client had confirmed that detailed evidence did not exist, and they had seen nothing to contradict the client's view. I explained to the court that I had attended their client's offices and reviewed the documents, discovering that in fact the evidence necessary for a fully particularised and substantiated claim was available. The judge ordered that a particularised claim be presented.

What, therefore, are Expert Witnesses to learn from a brief discussion of these psychological terms? In summary I believe we learn this.

- Human beings are programmed to defend their own psyche by the instinctive use of cognitive dissonance and confirmative bias.
- Some people will take these instinctive behaviours a step further and deliberately fail to recognise contradictory evidence.
- Experts are not inexorably bound by natural or instinctive human behaviours. Once understood, these behaviours can be overcome. By consciously seeking all of the facts and objectively examining them, Expert Witnesses are able to arrive at the real truth.

Armed with this snippet of knowledge, we may feel inclined to give opponents the benefit of the doubt when they have missed obvious evidence which potentially undermines their case, but any such benefit of the doubt must quickly dissipate if they refuse to accept that reliable evidence when it is plainly presented.

It is my view that honesty and integrity are the first two hallmarks of the truly unbiased expert witness. Two others are impartiality and independence.

2.8 Impartiality and Independence

If you are following the rules laid out above, you will already be impartial, and you will recognise the same impartiality in your opposing expert. Independence, however, has a slightly different connotation for an expert.

An independent expert witness means what it says. You should be independent of your instructing legal team and your client. You should also (perhaps more controversially) be independent of your own employer in matters of opinion.

Your opinion is yours alone. You may have relied on the work of others in the preparation of your report and the founding of your opinion, but the independently formed opinion is yours to defend. You will need to defend it against all-comers.

Here are some *fictitious* examples of how an expert could come under pressure to sacrifice their independence.

Client Pressure.

"Listen to me, you may be an expert reporting to a tribunal, but I am paying you. Your report is not helpful to me. But with a few tweaks here and there…"

The answer is first to stand firm and then respond with something like this.

"If I am not truly independent that will become obvious to the opposition and to the Tribunal. I will lose their confidence and the Tribunal will have only one independent evaluation to rely upon; their own. I believe that I have honestly and impartially evaluated your case. However, if my facts or analysis are wrong, my opinion may change. But it cannot change without a reason. To do so would result in you facing an award computed by the opposing expert, which will be far less generous than my evaluation."

No-one wants to disappoint a client, and cut off a potential future income stream, but most clients come around eventually. In my 28 years of working as an expert I have lost only two client companies when I refused to be swayed. One of these returned years later, the other faced a criminal investigation.

Legal Team Pressure

"If you were to be uncooperative in meetings and in any joint report, the controversial items could be left for us to argue out in the hearing, and we have the better advocate."

I have only once had legal team pressure applied to me and it was applied by lawyers from another jurisdiction who had never been in front of an international arbitration panel. I was removed as expert and my replacement subsequently lost the case badly, as my former opposing expert keeps reminding me every time we meet.

Legal teams are a wonderful resource to experts, not least because they can make a good report great by restructuring, or simply by editing. They also help experts by ensuring that the opinion is well founded and robust under questioning.

So, do not expect undue pressure from the legal team; it is exceedingly rare. If you do come across it, again hold fast to your true opinion and ask them to trust your former experience.

Employer Pressure

Occasionally pressure will be applied by your own employer. This is more likely if you work for a company which has other work streams with the same client. It will come in the form of 'handed down' pressure from others.

In such cases it is necessary for you to remember that the opinion is yours, not that of the company. You will be tested on it, they will not. If the case goes awry, they *will* run for the hills, you cannot.

In the 1990's, in the Technology and Construction Court (TCC) in front of a judge I knew well, the opposing party claimed that I had access to records that I had not disclosed. I was a little taken aback. It turned out that, unrecorded and without my knowledge, one of my company's former employees had worked on the project now in dispute. That employee had kept his own separate records and had discussed them with the opposition when everyone was still friendly. These documents were not in the general disclosure.

In a phone call I discovered that this employee had left before I joined the company and had taken long term work in Africa. The judge accepted that neither myself nor the legal team were to know of this data source, but he ordered that it be produced for the experts to review. This was a

Thursday afternoon, the last court sitting day of the week. The Judge wanted the documents by Monday.

After numerous calls to Nigeria I discovered that the documents were stored in a garage in the wilds of Northumberland. My company initially refused to cooperate, as they claimed that they had no control over the documents held by a former employee. I became exceeding unpopular at the office as I used my role as director to send a van and two assistant quantity surveyors to Northumberland on a Saturday on overtime.

We recovered the documents, which actually added nothing to the case, and the client picked up the bill for the document recovery efforts, and so all was well, but for a while I had to choose between the court and my employer.

Along with honesty and impartiality, your independence is something that you should treasure. As with everything else we value, we need to check regularly to ensure that it is still there, and intact.

Section 3:

Instructions and their Fulfilment

3.1 Winning Instructions

As is my wont, I am going to divert off topic before I even begin to discuss instructions. My Linked-In mailbox tends to fill with two types of query from fellow professionals. Firstly, "So, how do I become an Expert Witness?" my response being my Linked-In articles, podcasts, vlogs and this book.

The second most popular question I am asked is "How do I acquire instructions?" This is a complex question because there are many necessary components which will all contribute to a competent answer. Whilst this book is not specifically directed at the topic of selling expert services, I will give a brief overview of the *key* components as I see them, my five P's.

Personality: As a general rule, those chosen to testify in important cases will be partially chosen (even if subconsciously) on their personality. Thus.

- *Experts need to be confident, but not arrogant. If you stumble in your interview, you may stumble in your testimony. If you do, your honest, factual and genuinely useful opinion may appear halted and uncertain.*

I received my first expert instructions because my boss, a brilliant man whose work was exceptional and whose opinion was incontrovertible, was a nervous fellow. Public speaking was a challenge for him. He used beta-blockers to control his nervousness in some of his more important meetings. He never testified as an expert because the risk of his passing out was genuine, and that can be a real hindrance in a case with a tight timeline.

In a long running case in the TCC one of my opposing experts really did pass out on the stand, and only returned days later (very briefly) to give a truncated version of their testimony.

- *Experts need to be helpful, cooperative and friendly, avuncular even. You will get by with a stoic seriousness, but you will be more likely to impress clients if you are accessible.*

I am arguing here that clients are looking for people who present themselves as being *people-oriented* and *assertive*. Passives, passive-aggressives, aggressives and fact-oriented individuals all face additional challenges in cross examination. Some personality types can be provoked to anger quite quickly if they are doubted.

Popularity: This may seem a little shallow but, in my experience, the most successful experts I have encountered were popular. They may be popular because they are naturally charming, because they mix and network well, because they are entertaining or because they have found fame.

In my experience, previous success and fame are often strong ingredients in the expert instruction mix. Celebrate your previous experience, use social media, do not follow – be followed!

Presence: You need to be constantly at the forefront of the mind of your potential instructing lawyers. This is done by networking, volunteering help, advertising, marketing and just being a good friend.

Some years ago, as a company we placed a dozen calendars in the chambers of Judges in the TCC. These were inspirational calendars adorned with beautiful pictures and our company logo. As counsel, judges, clerks and others passed through the building they subliminally came to know that we were expert witnesses. How could they miss it?

Persistence: There is no substitute for persistence in seeking instructions. If one thing does not work, try another. Keep on keeping on. When I joined a new consultancy, I announced it by sending out over a hundred and fifty copies of a book 'Death of An Expert Witness' by P D James.

Along with it was a personal letter announcing the 'Birth of an Expert Witness Practice'. We received many phone calls and letters. There followed some very long-lasting relationships.

Pricing: Of course, pricing is important too. In my view those instructing experts should remember that:

$$Hours \times Rate = Price$$

Many clients become fixated on the cost of an expert's basic hourly rate but then end up paying a less expensive expert for many more hours than are needed, but at lower rates, still paying more overall.

A great expert like you will always find ways of resolving a client's problem efficiently without wasting either time or money. In Dubai, in 2014, a large developer refused to sign up to a well-known expert's hourly rate and hastily appointed another practice at a lower rate.

The expert they rejected was a busy man, an architect and a practicing arbitrator, who only ever charged for eight-hour days as he had so much work that he was obliged to work efficiently if he ever wanted to see his wife. If he worked more than eight hours in a day, he did not need to charge the client because he had already met his earning objective and covered his overheads in his hourly rate. His daily rate was £300 x 8 hours, £2,400 per day. The expert chosen by the developer operated a 'standard' 9.5-hour day policy at £250 per hour, or £2,375 per day, and they charged for any daily hours over 9 hours at full rate. That client might well have asked which was the better deal overall when the reporting deadlines often demanded 12-hour days?

As an expert witness you will need to help clients understand your pricing strategy and the synergies and efficiencies that you will bring to the work. It is for you to explain why you are more competitive overall.

When I first went into consultancy in the 1990's, our company pricing strategy was simply this:

- We estimated the annual number of hours we expected to expend earning fees.

- We calculated our annual salaries and all overheads, *including marketing and time spent marketing*.
- We divided the costs by the expected hours.
- Then we only applied the resources required for the work.
- Finally, we only worked the hours necessary for the work.

This meant that if we charged for the hours expected, we met our budget. If we worked less hours than expected we may take a loss against budget, but we still made a good living and had many grateful clients.

Sometimes, as expert deadlines approach, we are obliged by clients to work long hours, but if they are compensated with equivalent time off in lieu, we can still meet our financial and personal goals. Our intent should be to subsidise our inevitable 'downtime' without having to raise our rates or charge for every single hour worked and travelled.

This also allows experts the privilege of being able to carry out pro-bono assignments.

Admittedly, experts adopting this approach are unlikely to become millionaires, but we can help companies who perhaps could not afford a top expert otherwise, and we can still enjoy a quality of life that allows us ample family time.

In short, you can reduce stress and worry by being realistic about your annual fee earning hours, charging rates and time away from the office. But, beware, when busy, avarice can easily take hold and drive normally sensible individuals to work longer and harder than the case requires.

Hourly Rates

You can price your own time on the formula above, which in our case in 2020 brings our expert hourly rates to between £200 and £225 per hour, if we control our overheads, which we do. Given that one of my friends is paying freelance project QS's working on a power station in the Midlands up to £105 per hour, you can see that £200 per hour is easily justifiable in the UK for experts.

Obviously, the cost of employment increases dramatically if you are London based and need large or spacious offices. We are London office based, but much of our work is done at home or carried out in clients' premises around the world. I would expect our rates to rise to £300 per hour if we all had to be present in our London offices every day.

3.2 Instructions.

Back on track, I will now deal with instructions in all of their varieties.

In my experience, instructions come in every level of detail from none whatsoever, to extreme micromanagement listings. The reason for little or no detail in instructions may be that, on occasion, the legal team is uncertain what the true source of the dispute is.

If the source of the conflict is not a legal issue, it may fall outside their expertise. If that is so, then you may expect one of three things to happen:

You might commence with no instructions; you might commence with instructions that are outcome oriented rather than task oriented, or you may be invited to write your own instructions.

If you have no instructions or are invited to write your own instructions, just follow the advice below.

Task Oriented Instructions:

This is an approach adopted by lawyers who are experienced in this type of case and who are confident of their expert needs. They will remind you of the expert rules prevailing and that you are reporting and testifying to the Tribunal for the benefit of the Tribunal.

The instructions will then explain the case and the differences. You will be tasked, in writing, with answering or supporting the listed parts of the case. In this regard, your instructions are very much like a brief for an independent contractor; you will be told what to do but not how to do it.

If you find that the instructions are over-zealous in some areas and underwhelming in others, you are quite entitled to discuss any changes that may be required to best serve the client and inform the Tribunal.

Remember that you may be cross examined on your instructions, and your adherence to them, so you need to be ready for such questions or you need to ensure that you match the written instructions to your work.

This type of instructions may run to many pages and so they must be read carefully. Your clients and PI insurers would welcome your cooperation in this regard.

Objective Oriented Instructions

I had a friend who was a regional manager for a well-known burger chain. He was persistently being asked by a store manager to dismiss a store cleaner named Ronnie. Ronnie was a personable lad with learning difficulties. He was hard working and determined to make an honest living to support his new wife and child. Unfortunately, he seemed unable to rank his many duties in order of priority and so, on occasion, parts of the restaurant would become unkempt.

In his defence, Ronnie had a task list of almost 100 items that needed to be attended to regularly and as needed, and his reading skills were not stellar. My friend took Ronnie to one side.

"Ronnie, what is your mother-in-law like?" he asked.

"She's a tyrant, she is. Nothing is ever good enough for her," Ronnie said wide eyed.

"That is what I hear. Listen, Ronnie. For one week this is what you do. You clean the restaurant as if your mother-in-law is about to make an unannounced inspection. Then I come back and see the results."

The result was that Ronnie, freed from a list, kept that restaurant in pristine condition. Ronnie became objective oriented.

Objective oriented expert instructions work in the same way. They will essentially direct you to:

- Identify the areas where your expertise will be useful.
- Use standard, and acceptable protocols to execute your duties.
- Keep the client and legal team informed as to your findings.
- Prepare independent, readable and comprehensible reports.
- Behave professionally and assertively in meetings.
- Testify with conviction and humility.

Speaking as an expert who has been instructed in all possible ways on project disputes ranging from a few thousand pounds to over a billion pounds, I would always seek to settle my instructions early if I were you.

A set of instructions that give the expert the necessary scope to investigate and report, but which have reasonable limits, are also helpful to the testifying expert in cross examination.

I have one warning to issue in this section and it is this - if you receive firm instructions not to deal with a matter on which the Tribunal is seeking help, discuss it with your legal team and explain the potential downside. If they are insistent in their limitation and you decide to continue anyway, you must ensure that this exception is noted in both expert meetings and in the instructions section of your report.

Section 4:

The First Written Report

4.1 Introduction.

Before I begin, I need to make it clear that this section is compiled from my experiences of what courts and tribunals like to see in built environment and offshore cases. In different jurisdictions and in different specialisations these recommendations may not be appropriate. Some tips, however, are universal in their application and so should be useful to all.

There are a few basic rules that experts should bear in mind when writing any report:

- We are writing for the benefit of the reader, not our own ego.
- The reader will not necessarily be expert in our field.
- The reader is a busy man or woman.
- The report is intended to direct the reader towards acceptance of our opinion.
- Our report/ opinion will be challenged in front of the Tribunal.
- Human beings are unsettled by views or opinions that are entirely negative.
- Readers will understand that one side rarely has all of the truth on their side.

Some of these principles will guide our writing of the report, others will direct our formatting of the report. Let us begin with communication.

4.2 Communication

The essence of all reports is enlightenment. We expect to lift the reader from the foggy lowland mists of obfuscation onto higher ground where they can enjoy clarity and understanding. I may have been a little too poetic there, but you can see my point. We are essentially helping another individual to understand our complex professional world. In order to do this, we need to:

- Be concise.
- Be clear and precise.
- Avoid jargon and industry specific terms.
- Use simple language and good punctuation.

I am sure that your expert report will be a joy to read and that the tribunal would gladly set down the latest John Grisham novel and immerse themselves in your narrative instead, but you cannot rely on that happening.

In the main, society has come to rely on summaries, sound bites, headlines and synopses. Complex issues are dismissed on the national news in around two minutes, a global emergency might warrant a few more minutes. In a society like ours we cannot expect to hold anyone's attention for as long as we need it. So, we must learn to summarise our opinions and to be concise in our writing.

This can be done, and it carries real benefits. In one of my early cases the Judge followed the reasoning in my report and awarded a sum very close to my recommendation, which happened to be less than 30% of my opponent's evaluation. I then had to appear before a taxation master who had to decide whether my fees provided my client with value for money and whether to allow my client full reimbursement of my fees. The opposing lawyer took his expert's report and mine and laid them on a desk, pointing out that my report had cost twice as much as my opponent's report, which was twice as thick. The Judge acting as taxation master asked me for my view. I replied that if I had known they were going to weigh the reports rather than read them I would have used heavier paper. The taxation master laughed, the lawyer did not. My client was ultimately awarded my full fee because the trial Judge had relied on it so closely when making his award.

If *Readers Digest* can condense books down to around half of their original length, and *Audible.com* can abridge books to a third of the unabridged listening time, then we can probably reduce our reports without losing clarity.

One way of reducing the bulk of your report is by extracting tables, charts, quotations, spreadsheets and databases and creating appendices for them, thus making the narrative more accessible. Another tip is the executive summary and the law of three. There is a theory in psychological circles that short term memory is assisted by repetition. They assert that if a fact is repeated three times in 72 hours it is likely to be converted into long term memory. So, whilst keeping the document concise you should:

1. Tell them what you are going to tell them.
2. Tell them.
3. Tell them that you told them.

This is, in essence, how Tribunals work. The opening statement says, 'this is the case I will prove', the evidence is then provided as the case is heard, and the closing argument says 'this is the case I have proven.

In a report we can address these three points as follows:

1. Provide an executive summary at the outset.
2. Then, explain your research, methodology, analysis and findings.
3. Finally, include your reasoned conclusions and opinions in a separate section at the end.

I have witnessed many instances where decision makers have done little more than read the conclusions and findings in a report, so make sure they can be found easily and quickly.

Being concise is important but so is being clear. There is danger in not being clear in our views. I read a report from a technical expert who described in detail seven methods of approaching a problem. I had lost the will to live after method number four. However, this was not the worst aspect of the report. The technical expert did not provide a summary and so it was for the reader to trawl back through all seven methods to discern their merits and determine which the expert preferred and why. The danger for his client was that this expert was right but that his opinion was unfathomable, whilst the opposition's much simpler report was wrong but readily understandable. You can see where a Tribunal may struggle in this situation.

The only way of being entirely sure that your report is concise yet clear is to have a peer review. You must allow someone of *equal standing* to critique it. If you do so you will be surprised how paragraphs which were clear to you a few short hours ago are now incomprehensible. Read the following paragraph from a real report.

"In my opinion the PRV scans resonate over a superior fractal spectrum and in my view the increased functionality creates a definable improvement over the entire dimensional perspective, assuming that x^n => y^n in ambient temperatures. So, it is my opinion that the Tribunal should accept this methodology."

Sorry, you lost me at the fifth word, what is a PRV scan? Tribunals are laymen as far as we are concerned. They need our world explaining to them. We must begin by explaining what we are seeking to test, explore and value. We must explain our methodology and why we have selected that methodology. We must then explain the results and their reliability, stating any concerns or caveats clearly. Everything must be explained.

Acronyms, unusual expressions, specific use of generic words all must be contained in a glossary or avoided. A surgeon who describes a patient who has *voided* his bowels means he emptied his bowels, a lawyer who says his client *voided* a contract means that the contract has legally ceased to exist. Many common words or expressions will have a vastly different meaning to different professions, and so care is required in explaining exactly what we mean, in language that the reader can understand without misinterpretation.

We also need to be careful with punctuation. Remember the book that showed us how not to punctuate; *Eats shoots and leaves* by Lynne Truss. We know that a Panda *eats shoots and leaves*, whereas, a murderous houseguest *eats, shoots, and leaves* but all too often our punctuation, or lack of it, causes ambiguity.

4.3 Format

The format of your report will be dependent upon your discipline and your tribunal. Nonetheless, some rules must be followed.

- Title page with parties' names, case number and the nature and title of your report. Be sure to make sure the Tribunal know by whom you are instructed.
- Contents page if length demands it.
- Introduce yourself.
- Introduce your instructions.
- Explain your understanding of the facts.
- Explain your methods but be sure to start at the beginning.
- Explain your findings, conclusions and opinion.
- Sign off by declaring your honesty and independence.
- Append your CV and any other documents necessary to support your report.

4.4 Psychology of the Reader

You need to win over the reader. You want him to agree with you and so you need to adopt some simple procedures.

- Be respectful and polite in your report.
- Be balanced. Tribunals are experienced in life and in their professions and will not easily accept that one party is entirely in the right and the other is entirely in the wrong.
- Mention the weaknesses in your instructing party's case and discuss them, reaching a conclusion about each.

- Do not provide an entirely negative report, seeking only to destroy the opposition's case. Ensure that you contrast your positive case with theirs and entice the tribunal to accept your positive case.
- Give the Tribunal no reason to dislike you. (Bias, pride, ego, rudeness, know it all etc.)

If the Tribunal like you and believe that you are appropriately qualified or experienced, they will listen to your case more readily.

4.5 Presentation.

Finally, presentation is important. I always use loose leaf ring binders so that the reader can access individual pages. I comb bound my first report with fabulous coloured graphics on the front page and company logo prominently placed. When I arrived at counsel's office to review my report, he had stripped the binding, punched holes and put my report in a scruffy third hand lever arch file with two earlier case names carelessly scribbled out. I learned my lesson.

Professional presentation suggests professional content.

Section 5:

Meetings, Discussions and Agreements

5.1 Introduction

A few years ago, I suffered the worst possible start to a new expert witness relationship. I had flown to the West Coast of the USA to meet with an opposing expert, and whilst I was in the air the lawyers exchanged our initial expert reports. When I arrived at the opposition expert's offices the morning after landing, I received a frosty reception, nothing new there. Experts are often initially considered to be just another battalion in the opposition's army, at least until we become acquainted. I was politely ushered into a conference room with a large table surrounded by a dozen chairs. A few minutes later an extremely angry man entered the room. His face was bright red and contorted with rage. He threw down a sheaf of papers and asked, "What the hell is this?" It was a print-out of my report.

Before I could answer, he embarked on an expletive ridden monologue that accused me of insulting his integrity, defiling his company and, by association, disrespecting the whole of the USA. He then grabbed a chair and threw it in my general direction.

Even my expert poker face must have displayed some puzzlement. He then stormed out. I waited. Where was there to go? His colleagues appeared and explained that he was angry because I had heavily criticised their beautifully crafted report and, as the main author, he felt slighted.

I asked them to look at my report and their own report and read the dates. My report had preceded their report. I had not seen their report yet. It was delivered to me by email overnight. They soon realised that my report had critiqued their client's claim, not their expert report. Once the penny dropped, the little group looked bashful. I later received a sincere apology from the expert himself who sat beside his wife, also an expert witness, as he admitted to her and to me that he had not been taking his recommended medications and had a terrible journey into work.

When we parted later that day all was well as we had discovered we had a lot in common. That expert witness remains a good friend to this day.

I do not relate this story to scare you, but to show you that no matter how bad the meeting begins, it can eventually lead to good results.

Another example of meetings gone wrong, came from my time as a young Commercial Director for an international construction company, I was heading up European Sales and Projects. Some of these sales were in Eastern Europe where the potential clients/ government could not pay us in cash, let alone in sterling. To acquire these projects, we had to think outside the box and so we employed a banker, a man of maturity, experienced in commodities trading. Thus, we would construct a project and be paid in trees or wheat or whatever else they produced. As a bonus, we often made more from trading the commodities on the London Commodities Markets than we did from designing, manufacturing and constructing the project itself.

The commodities trader was a nice guy, very sociable and so he loved to 'visit', often when I was busy. I was always patient with him because I knew that others were often not as kindly. However, he had an odd habit that could easily drive a sane person to distraction, he loved using sayings, or analogies to explain his point of view. The problem was that the 'sayings' were neither in popular use, nor understandable.

After one discussion he said, enigmatically, 'To me it's like cooking potatoes, you boil a pan of potatoes and you don't add a pinch of salt.' Pause for dramatic effect. 'You have wasted a pound of potatoes and twenty minutes of your life for the lack of a pinch of salt.' There were so many flaws in the analogy that I had to let it go, I had no wish to still be engaged in this conversation when darkness set in, and it was already 10am.

As time went on, more and more sayings were cited, each more meaningless than the last, and so I tried a different tactic. Before he could sign off with one of his homilies, I would offer one of my own.

At the end of our next meeting I piped up with my first foray into the genre: 'As my father used to say, if it isn't already pretty, don't paint it yellow.' Now my father never offered anything as silly or meaningless as this as advice, and I thought perhaps I had gone too far. Not so. The man looked studious and responded: 'That is very deep, do you mind if I use it?' It was then that I knew I was in for the long haul.

Over the next weeks I had to spend my evenings creating ever more ridiculous sayings, as each and every one of my previous nonsensical maxims was openly accepted as a finely polished pearl of wisdom. There followed such classics as:

'You can sandpaper walls, but you can't wallpaper sand!', and, 'As Confucius says, it is easier to slide down the neck of a scaly dragon than to climb up it.'

All to no avail. Eventually I had to bite the bullet and insist on an agenda and a limited time for each meeting, explaining that we shouldn't be having so much fun when others were working hard.

Meetings of all kinds can be difficult and so we need to adopt a proven approach, especially when we are perceived as being party who would benefit most from an agreement. So, on a more serious note let us examine some of the key issues driving consensus.

5.2 Common Ground

The real purpose of expert meetings is to discover common ground and to attempt to narrow the issues that are currently before the Tribunal. The areas where there are unexplained differences in opinion usually dictate the agenda and these may be as follows:

1. You may be relying on data, information or records that are different from those relied upon by the opposing expert.

2. You may be using different methodologies to analyse the data.
3. Your interpretation of the data may differ.
4. Your prognosis of the outcome may differ even if you agree all three of the above.

If you want to find out if and where you differ, the suggestions above should form the basis of an agenda. Misunderstanding and mistrust may well have fuelled the original dispute. Do not let them flourish during the expert process.

5.3 First Things First

As with all meetings and negotiations, we must remember that we are in discussions with another human being who has all the frailties we ourselves enjoy. They encounter health issues, family problems, economic challenges, mechanical failures and so on. Some experts are fabulous at their profession but are hopeless communicators, others are deeply eccentric. They may not share the same values, principles or interests as us. Their pastimes or hobbies may seem alien to us. The artwork in their offices may be differ widely from our taste in art.

For all of these reasons we need to enter into discussions armed with tolerance, patience and forbearance. We must try to remain calm in the stormiest meeting.

My personal approach is to try to build rapport and make a friend. At this point, I do have to admit that opposing experts constitute a worryingly high proportion of my friends. We generally establish rapport by:

- Smiling.
- Being amiable.
- Asking about our counterpart and their interests.
- Finding common ground or common friends/lawyers/contacts.

It is likely that an opposing expert will be from a similar discipline. They may have similar education and experiences, they may be from the same ethnic, racial, or religious background. They may support the same football team as you. Any commonality at all will help to build rapport. If you find that you have little in common, remember that you probably have extraordinarily little in common with some of your close friends, too. This is because so often opposites attract.

Twenty years ago, I travelled to Birmingham to the HQ of a government body. My intent was to negotiate the financial close-out of a project with my team. As we sat down the two teams chatted amiably until the opposing negotiator entered the room. He looked cross. Perhaps he always looked cross. He took charge of the conversation and began with this speech.

"I have read your book about manipulating people, by building rapport and becoming friends. Well, it will not be happening here today. You and I will not be having a cosy lunch, swapping anecdotes and sharing snapshots of our families. This negotiation will be tough and uncompromising."

The room fell silent, not least because his assistant had booked a separate table at lunchtime for the two lead negotiators at a nice restaurant close by.

I sat and thought for a moment. I really needed to do nothing because my opposing negotiator had just given away his entire game plan before we had begun.

"I agree," I said in response. "We should just move on and forget all of that rapport building nonsense. We can respect each other for our skills without forcing a friendship." He smiled, a little triumph for him at the very beginning of the day.

I spent the rest of the day building rapport, in the same way as usual, subtly and successfully. At the end of the day we shook hands and he said, "I bet that was the hardest negotiation you have had for a long time." I replied that he surely was 'one of a kind' and left with everything we had hoped for, and more.

That man was a wonderful guy who I met many times afterwards. He just needed affirmation that he was in charge. As an expert you will need to be a student of human behaviour, and later in your career you will need to be able to read a room.

However, it is to be achieved, once we are happy that both experts are calm and relaxed, we move to the agenda.

5.4 Dealing with Data

Expert meetings will suffer from a slow start if we are not opining on common data. It is often the case that we have seen documents or data that our expert counterpart has not. Likewise, they will be privy to information we have not seen.

So please underline this next piece of crucial advice. It is neither clever nor responsible to conceal data that would reduce conflict and so all relevant information should be disclosed. My preference is to reveal all data early, rather than hijack the opposition with a surprise revelation later. To do so is mean-spirited and it will gain you no ground in the long term. Be on you best behaviour. You are being observed.

If possible, experts should agree a common data set, or if that is not possible, they should at least agree the contents of both data sets. This at least removes potential arguments about shifting data.

In some cases, the dispute may entirely arise from the question of whether one set of data is accurate or whether the other data set is more reliable. If this is the case the experts should comment on both data sets so that when the tribunal decides which data set is correct, they have both experts' opinions on that data set.

5.5 Methodology

Once we have managed the data, we will have to review it or analyse it to come to an opinion of what it means in terms of the case pleaded. There are often many ways to analyse the data but hopefully the experts can decide on one industry standard methodology. This is not always possible.

If it is not, then I suggest the following approach in meetings:

1. Explain why you prefer your method.
2. Listen to why they prefer their method.
3. See if you can agree either method.
4. If not, agree to evaluate each other's methodology.

This way the Tribunal can decide on which dataset to allow and which methodology to use, knowing that each expert has tested the accepted dataset and methodology.

Always be aware that you do not have to agree to a methodology that you believe is flawed, you just have to ensure that the opposing expert has applied his chosen method correctly.

In delay disputes there are many potential analytical methodologies or tools. If you choose one be sure to have a robust defence of your use of that methodology. You must also ensure that the methodology chosen is appropriate for the data available and the circumstances in which it is to be applied. Reference to protocols, rules, standard methodologies and learned texts are fine but you are the expert, you must convince the tribunal that the method, however widely acclaimed, is appropriate in this specific case.

Five years ago, I was instructed on a quantum case in the USA where the opposing expert chose a global approach to evaluation. It was in the usual form of:

Total Expenditure – Expected Expenditure = Loss

His client was seeking over $500 million in damages. We both agreed that this was not going to pass muster with a tribunal and so the opposing expert set about preparing, and justifying, a modified global claim. The essence of the modified version of the global claim was that each element or head of claim, would be a mini global claim. Admittedly, when this was done tens of millions dropped out of the claim to my client's benefit, but each mini claim was still worth tens of millions of dollars and was still being calculated on a total loss basis.

The next step the expert took was to support each mini global claim with evidence and some degree of particularisation. This was done well initially but because the expert was lacking in factual data (actually, he was overwhelmed by hundreds of thousands of pages of data in Portuguese) he extrapolated.

I pointed out the frailty of the methodology in expert meetings and gave my opinion that in an expert report any methodology must be based on the data available. The expert should not find a method approved by learned texts and try to shoehorn existing data into it.

At the hearing, the expert gave a wonderful slide show on how the costs had arisen and had been valued. When he sat down the tribunal consulted and had only one question. "How does your methodology demonstrate the real losses attached to each cause?" He could not answer convincingly and had a torrid time in cross examination and hot tubbing.

In a later Middle East case a well-known arbitrator was assigned to direct the quantum experts, who were struggling to value the varied options the two delay experts were offering to the tribunal. As he spoke to the two of us, he gave some wonderful advice that I pass on to you.

An expert should choose an acceptable method and implement it as it was meant to be implemented. To stray from the accepted approach is to undermine the model in the eyes of the tribunal.

5.6 Findings

Life would be much simpler if once we had agreed the dataset and the methodology, the experts found that their findings were the same, but that would be too easy, and everyone would want to be an expert witness.

It is so often the case that results derived from methodically analysing the datasets still demand interpretation and so become subjective.

On a recent case I calculated a profit percentage of 6.05% was due. Using similar data and methodology my counterpart calculated 5.15%. In normal circumstances this would not be a problem but the capital sum in question was £500m, meaning that a 1% difference was equal to £5m. We sat together in a meeting and reviewed our interpretation of the results and constructed a common set of criteria for *interpreting* the data that we could both agree was reasonable. The calculation was run again using the agreed criteria and 5.75% was the figure we arrived at and agreed.

Again, if you cannot agree the figure, just ensure that you can both explain eloquently why your interpretation should be preferred.

5.7 Opinion

Once you have agreed the findings or reached a conclusion you are happy to defend, your opinion should be straightforward. If both expert witnesses are honest and open there should be little disharmony, even if their opinions differ. By reporting independently and honestly, you will find the correlation between expert opinions to be much improved.

Try to offer an opinion to the tribunal that gives some certainty to their decision. Try not to offer too many alternatives. Alternatives that have been properly disregarded by the experts, as a result of applying their expertise, need not be presented to the tribunal. If they are presented, they may cause confusion. "Why offer us an option that you have discounted?" they may ask.

In Kuwait, some years ago now, a project was terminated early and the work completed had to be valued. I had been instructed by the claimant and they were happy to be confined by the contract rates, to keep the claim simple and save dispute costs. So, the real dispute was the measurement of work completed at termination. There was no real dispute as to the Bills of Quantities or the schedule of rates for work completed.

However, in negotiations the two parties now in dispute had presented a 'simplified' BoQ to the client, who contracted on that basis. The parties then sought to contract between themselves. It was not made clear whether they were contracting on the original (accurate) BoQ or the simplified (approximate) BoQ.

The approximate version had been derived from the accurate version by removing/undervaluing many necessary items that were unlikely to change from the BoQ and spreading the Contract Value over the remaining items. Clearly this would make the remaining items more expensive and might be considered unfair because thereafter all variations using those rates would be overpriced.

Naturally, the experts were unhappy with the simplified BoQ because it did not reflect the real bargain or reflect real measurements or prices. Each expert discussed it with their client and legal team, and all agreed that the original BoQ should be used by their experts.

I presented one option for evaluation, using the agreed data and a single methodology. My opposing expert, possibly to show how hard he had worked for his client, presented five options, one of which was mine.

In his opinion section he set about dismissing my option and two others as inferior. He then hovered between two of his five options.

The Tribunal were upset at having so many options before them and asked us to leave the hearing and settle on one each, maximum. The opposing expert would not do so, and we returned to the Tribunal, who showed no emotion but clearly felt some.

One of the options my opponent had discussed n his report was pricing the measured work at simplified BoQ rates, thus giving a figure 20%

higher than the figure I was offering to the Tribunal. He then set about dismissing this 'overvalued' option with relish, somehow suggesting that my client was being dishonest in preparing such a document, even though they were not claiming on that basis.

Unfortunately for my opponent, in testimony under oath, the opposition Project Manager admitted that he had instructed the simplified BoQ. Thus, muddying the waters.

To cut a long story a little shorter, the Tribunal reviewed that testimony and, because they had my opponent's inflated valuation based on the simplified BoQ to hand, they allowed it. My client enjoyed a windfall of over £5 million, when compared to my valuation based on the original, accurate BoQ.

Had the opposing expert not offered five options, three of which he did not accept anyway, the Tribunal could only have awarded either my evaluation which was £5 million lower than their actual award, or my opponent's preferred evaluation, which was £20 million lower again.

My advice is this. Once experts have simplified the evaluation options, discard the other rejected options and produce a joint report with only the agreed options in place. You might just save you client several million pounds.

Section 6:

The Final Report & Joint Reports

6.1 Introduction

Long before I became an expert witness, I was a QS, Commercial Manager and later a Commercial Director for three different contracting entities. When I was Commercial Manager for an international building controls company, I didn't have to negotiate too much at all because there were only two or three major players in the market and none of us would accept the standard terms and conditions of our clients, including the ubiquitous pay-when-paid clauses. We had an industry standard, fair set of conditions that we would each tailor to a client's needs. When they agreed to honour these terms, they were incentivised by bonuses and discounts. It worked well.

However, earlier in my career, when I was in M&E subcontracting as a Commercial Director, the market was large and negotiations on terms were tough. You had to be slick and fleet of foot to survive in an incredibly competitive environment.

6.2 Back in Time

In 1988, when dealing with one quite renowned client, who had blazed the trail on imposing unlimited set-off clauses, I became aware of their propensity for setting-off unattributed monies from the sums properly due to their contractors. The client would comply with the Contract as it had been constructed in terms of certification, but then they would make a deduction for set-off, citing a variety of spurious causes. The client had famously hired a powerful lawyer to draft these contracts and their assistant replicated them for project after project. There was much case law on these types of contracts in the 1980's and 1990's.

In this turbulent period, I had been negotiating the contract terms for a major contracting organisation with this powerful lawyer's assistant, and then the final detailed wording was negotiated with the client's in-house lawyer. The only clause upon which we could not agree was what appeared to me to be an unlimited set-off clause. It read something like this.

"In the event that any loss or cost is incurred by the client due to the acts, omissions, or any other failure of the contractor, the client shall be entitled to set off, from any sums due and payable, any sums for which they are liable."

I have to admit that if pushed I can be as sneaky and underhand as the next man. My discussion on this clause went something like this.

"How do we know that the sum for which we are supposedly liable is not the fault of other contractors, or no-one at all?" I asked.

"We will only deduct sums properly calculated by us, as being due for your errors," was the answer.

"In your judgement?" I asked innocently. "Yes," was the reply.

"OK then. Let us explain that in the clause, which would now read. '"In the event that any loss or cost is incurred by the client due to the acts, omissions, or any other failure of the contractor, the client shall be entitled to set off, from any sums due and payable, any sums for which they are *judged* liable."

The wording was instantly agreed, and the Contract was signed. Four months into the Contract the client tried to set-off a huge amount of money unfairly, citing the set off clause. I wrote to the client and their lawyers in this vein.

"With regard to the alleged right to set-off, the plain and clear words of the Contract state that you can only set-off when we have been *judged* liable for the set-off. In recent case law, a Judge in the Official Referees Court restated a long-standing legal principle that I remember well from my law degree. Judgements on liability are the sole territory of the judiciary. You cannot deduct set-off without a Judge deciding on liability when the explicit wording says 'judged liable'."

The client and their legal team were incensed and took the money anyway. I wrote a letter and hand delivered it to the originating lawyer. In it I asked them to review the law and advise the client in light of the existing law, making payment immediately.

We received payment in full that day and for the remainder of the project, but not before I received an angry letter alleging that I had been underhand and had taken advantage of the in-house counsel's good will. Clearly our definitions of good will differed widely.

6.3 Say what you mean to say!

I tell this story because it highlights an unworthy display of deceit from one party who wants to persuade you that the words may explicitly say that they will take your money without citing a good reason, but in reality they would never do such a thing without talking it through. Yes, they would, and when you complained they would point you to the Contract.

We should never agree wording in Contracts or in Expert Reports that do not accurately reflect the whole intent of the parties.

I offer this as a warning. It is my experience that experts and those instructing them are almost always honourable and fair, but some are not. I have seen many cases where narrative traps have deliberately been set in Joint Reports that were then alighted upon in cross examination. Read everything carefully and seek advice if the wording you are being asked to accept appears unusually legalistic or odd. It may not be as innocent as it appears.

6.4 Experts should be open with one another.

In the early 2000's I was an expert witness in a long running Technology and Construction Court case which involved major project delay and the recovery of the attendant costs. The judge requested that the two experts prepare a spreadsheet that showed the differences between us and citing where he could find our supporting opinions in our final reports.

To my surprise the opposing expert sent me a note saying he would draft the spreadsheet and submit it to me for my agreement. I was immediately suspicious because the expert was an elderly gent who had always eschewed technology in the past. Nonetheless, I waited for his spreadsheet. It arrived very late on a Sunday night and the hearing recommenced on Monday morning. My agreement was sought by 8:30am the next day.

The spreadsheet was large, cumbersome and complex. It was not particularly intuitive either. Discovering bias and inaccuracy throughout, overnight I exported the factual data onto a new, slicker spreadsheet. I then set about filling in the descriptive boxes honestly, from the two final reports. I sent both reports to my counsel with a note from me on the opposition's version of the spreadsheet, which was wildly biased and often critical of my work.

The judge asked for the spreadsheet and was given two different versions. He was unhappy. When he asked my counsel why I had not simply agreed the opposition's spreadsheet, my counsel led the tech savvy judge through the spreadsheet.

Judges know how experts phrase their opinions and how lawyers phrase theirs. He saw before him a very legalistic spreadsheet. Counsel used my crib sheet to lead the judge through the origins of the spreadsheet. According to the properties dialogue box it originated in the lawyers' offices on Thursday evening, it was amended in the lawyers' offices over the weekend and final changes were made on Sunday, and the document was printed at the lawyers' offices.

Opposing counsel noted that his instructions were that the lawyers prepared the template and that the expert filled the boxes as ordered. He then stated that he took no responsibility for the spreadsheet. It was the work of others.

The Judge asked one question of the opposing expert who was in the body of the courtroom. "Where were you on Sunday?" The expert confirmed that he was out of contact in Hertfordshire with his family at the time the changes were being made.

The judge pointedly asked the opposition if they could agree my spreadsheet, as the court would prefer one agreed document. Opposing counsel agreed immediately without consulting his expert or his instructing solicitors, who gamely tried to attract his attention but who were silenced by junior counsel.

Trickery and misbehaviour lead, inevitably, to disaster. Don't be tempted to cheat. Your reputation is worth more than that.

6.5 Joint Reports

Having now set the scene for you and having prepared you for potential pitfalls in joint reporting, let me take you through the process of joint reporting, done properly.

It is likely that when both reports are set side by side there will be areas of agreement. There will be areas where the disagreement can be overcome with discussion and sensible agreements. We are not there to compromise, of course, but everyone will benefit if we compromise wisely. The costs of disputing some small items can eclipse the difference in value. Finally, there will be differences where the gulf is too great to overcome.

Most of our clients are commercially minded. They understand the break even point better than we do. In my experience, most will readily accept paths to resolution that do not compromise their overall case, and which save time and money.

Compromise is not always necessary to reach agreement. Here are a few methods I have seen used in dispute resolution before and during the hearing stage.

Trends

If there are a great many changes to be priced by the experts and some are of low value, one possible way of reducing costs is to look at trends. So, you agree to value all of the variations/changes in excess of $5,000.00, and to do so with precision. Then you compare the value of those variations as priced by the experts with the value in the claim. If the value of the items over $5,000.00 is an average of 87% of the claimed value, you apply that same percentage to the many items below $5,000.00

If the limits are set wisely you can reduce the workload dramatically, saving tens of thousands of dollars on fees whilst clearing up hundreds, or thousands, of small items whose total value will not make or break the case.

Trading Off

In many cases claims are met by an equal and equivalent of counterclaims. When these are final valued, at great expense, the difference can be small or non-existent.

It is possible, with wisdom, to look at the merits of these claims and counterclaims and, if there is a liability, perhaps one credible item can be traded off against another, reducing the expert evaluation and saving fees.

In an offshore case my client would not agree trade-off the electrical works element of the dispute, even though the differences were minor, the works had been properly ordered, and that portion of the dispute was less than 2% of the overall dispute.

The experts each spent two weeks remeasuring and pricing the works to conclude that we were $27,000.00 apart, recognising that the Tribunal would probably have to split it anyway. We had each expended $30,000.00 to arrive at a position where we agreed that we were $27,000.00 apart, a quarter of a percent of the overall difference in dispute.

Anticipating the Tribunal

When faced with two great experts who disagree on the evaluation of delay or cost, and when liability has been settled, what can the Tribunal add? Probably nothing. They can only apportion the difference, possibly 50/50.

One method adopted by me and my opposing expert on a major Middle East dispute was the provision of an interactive spreadsheet.

We created a spreadsheet with all of the differences in time and money shown on a three-dimensional spreadsheet. When the Tribunal decided on a period of delay, they simply plotted the Extension of Time (EoT) into the allotted box. Then the spreadsheet recalculated the overall delay and the damages. When the Tribunal agreed liability on a change, they simply placed a *1* in the box for liability proven or *0* for disallowed. The spreadsheet also offered two valuations for every item on which the experts disagreed. The tribunal could then split the difference by rating the difference in value 1 to 100. Less than 50% favoured the respondent, greater than 50% favoured the claimant.

This spreadsheet took a few days to prepare and accelerated the Tribunal decision by weeks, if not months.

Ingenuity

Using your own ingenuity, and with the propensity experts have for innovation, I am sure that you will find many more ways of reaching equitable, if not always readily accepted, solutions to seemingly intractable disputes.

If the experts make progress with the support of the clients, the tribunals will not stand in the way, usually.

Bear this in mind. Whilst you may have prepared a number of reports between you, the Tribunal's first port of call for expert evidence will be the Joint Report.

To this end you need to ensure these three things:

1) The joint report accurately and fairly represents your findings.
2) The joint report should have as little narrative as possible, with all narrative being in clear, understandable, and unambiguous language.
3) The joint report should rely, as far as clarity allows, upon summary level graphics and spreadsheets.

If you follow these rules, where they are appropriate, you will find that the joint reporting process will be quicker, agreement will be easier, and outsiders will have less influence in the signed document.

It is possible that one, or both experts, will come under pressure to word things differently, or perhaps move emphasis in a specified direction. Both experts need to be strong, perhaps even implacable.

6.6 Final Reports

Dependent upon the individual process, the final report you write could precede the Joint Report or may come afterwards.

However, and whenever, it is served, your final report must fulfil the criteria of any other report, as described herein. That is:

a) It must be clear, concise, and certain.
b) It must explain its purpose, fulfil its purpose, and summarise its purpose in an opinion.
c) It must be presented well and equably. It must not be entirely negative.

This may be your final chance to influence the tribunal, prior to a hearing. Also remember that a great many cases will settle before a hearing, and so your final report may become a key negotiating document.

Section 7:

Preparation and Testifying

7.1 Introduction

This section becomes relevant when the final reports have been served and any joint statements have been finalised. You will then encounter the three distinct stages of trial preparation.

1) Personal preparation.
2) Expert Team preparation.
3) Legal Team preparation.

7.2 Personal Preparation

I begin my personal preparation by making a list of all the tasks I believe an expert should complete before testifying. The list is a simple one but if you have not prepared for a hearing before it may be helpful. I usually prepare for testifying in the same way that I prepared for my Professional exams and Law Degree exams.

This is my list, but you will have your own ideas and practices. Use mine as a guide or to backfill any gaps in your own list. These tasks do not have to be executed in order, and often they are carried out intermittently or are interspersed with other items later in the list. When you prepare for your first hearing you will understand exactly what I mean.

Tasks

a) Assemble, order, and catalogue all evidence relied upon, quoted, referenced, or used (however obliquely) in arriving at your opinion. This includes work product that was carried out, but which was later discarded. It is vital that you can trace back all decision-making processes to their source. You can legitimately be cross examined on analyses or exercises that were prepared but never used. You may even have to explain why the exercises were carried out and why the results were rejected/not used.

You can settle the tribunal and unsettle opposing counsel with a great explanation as to why work product was rejected. By following this procedure, you leave no doubts lingering in the minds of the tribunal.

b) Summarise all evidence and append brief notes that will act as an aide memoire. This may take the form of a contents list, possibly on a spreadsheet or in a simple database. In electronic form it can be hyperlinked to original documents and early research for quick access when you are alone and 'boxed'. This element of the preparation work can be carried out by a trusted assistant. As the trial date closes in I usually create ever more compact summaries until the day before the hearing. I am referring only to bullet points on a few sheets of A4, rather than the documents themselves.

c) Review your own report and ensure that all references are correct and easy to find in a witness box. Ask an expert witness colleague to read through your reports as well. Both of you can then prepare a list of potentially tough cross examination questions.

d) Do the same for the opposing reports and the joint report.

e) Role play your testimony with the questions raised in the former steps, ensuring that there is tension in the room. Choose a room with which you are unfamiliar and ensure the questioning is robust. Make the role play as real as possible.

f) Review the outcome of the role play and deal with the disasters - there will be some. Better to review and implement improvement now than be caught out on the day.

g) Relax, do what you enjoy, take time away from your desk. Rest, make sure your sleep pattern is settled. Eat lightly, avoid alcohol. Be wary of beta blockers or other 'calming' medications, they often leave a mark on your sharpness and memory processes.

h) Choose your clothes well in advance. Don't be distracted on the day.

i) Smile, exercise, release those endorphins. Use mantras and mindfulness if that is your thing but leave the Goat Yoga until the hearing is over.

7.3 Expert Team Preparation

Testifying will differ between Tribunals and Civil and Criminal cases. My practice has been in all three and so I comment generically about procedure. I have also testified in different jurisdictions around the world and so I make generalised comments about that experience too.

Having said that there are many differences between hearings, there are many more things which remain relatively constant, for example:

- In some cases, you will be able to sit in on the hearing until your testimony is due, while on other occasions you will not be allowed in the room until the tribunal allows it.
- The court or tribunal will ask you to confirm that your evidence will be honest. Some will ask you to swear an oath or affirm, others will take you at your word.
- They will usually ask you to confirm your identity, address, workplace and experience.
- You will be asked if your opinion has changed since you wrote your report. If you have noticed errors during preparation, this is your last opportunity to notify the tribunal.
- Your report may be accepted as your *examination in chief,* or you may be questioned by your instructing lawyers advocate.

- The opposing counsel will then have an opportunity to question you in *cross examination*. They may be harsher than your own counsel. They will undoubtedly be trickier.
- The judge or tribunal may also ask questions.
- If the tribunal breaks whilst you are in the witness chair, you will be 'boxed', that is; you will not be able to discuss the case with ANYONE outside the hearing until you have been released as a witness.
- Once released you are free to sit with your legal team and prepare questions for the opposition witnesses.

7.4 The Court or Arbitration Experience

It is likely that you will be nervous before testifying. If you are not, I suggest you check your wrist for a pulse, as you may have passed away! I have testified many times, and, on every occasion, I have been fully prepared and yet mildly terrified. The secret is acknowledging the nerves but not allowing them to freeze your brain or garble your speech.

You will probably enjoy the benefit of having your by now familiar written report before you, along with a kindly clerk eager to find any document you are referred to by counsel. Nonetheless, courts and arbitration rooms can be scary places. I have found that most courts are open to the public, so if you are concerned go along and sit in on an unrelated case, look around, familiarise yourself with the courtroom and the procedure, stay until you feel comfortable. Arbitration rooms are often open long before and after the hearing day, and so a quiet hour spent sitting relaxing in the witness chair can be therapeutic and beneficial later.

I am assuming here that you are well prepared and that you know your case well, as this is the best way to neutralise counsel's aggressive and detailed questions.

Arbitrations and many lower courts now have a relaxed dress code. Usually experts, counsel, lawyers and the tribunal are in lounge suits. In higher courts you may still encounter wigs, but almost always you will meet robed advocates, judges and clerks.

Naturally, you are expected to dress smartly and professionally, regardless of gender. Men will usually wear ties if they are wearing a collared shirt, albeit I have seen an increase in the wearing of polo shirts by witnesses of fact and some experts. There is no need to overdress. Try to dress as comfortably as you can. You do not need distractions.

In most tribunals you will be speaking into a microphone (largely for the benefit of the stenographer) and so you can adopt a normal conversational tone. Water is usually provided, and you can ask for a break at any time without the tribunal thinking any the worse of you.

7.5 Testifying

Relax and remember that you know your report better than anyone else, much better than the opposing counsel, or at least you should. Assuming that you do, the only way you will be caught out is if your report is contradictory or wrong. If you feel that you are being pressured into giving an answer that may be erroneous, try using one of these phrases:

- I wonder if I can look at my report/ document X before answering that question. I would not want to mislead the court.
- I cannot seem to find the reference. Could someone help me to find it please?
- That question is beyond my remit, but it is within my experience if the tribunal would like me to answer.
- That question is beyond my remit and outside my experience. My answer would be no more than that of a lay person.
- I cannot answer that question, I was not present/ have no personal knowledge of it, I have been working from the documents.
- That is a hypothetical question and I feel uncomfortable about answering it without stating clearly that my answer will also be hypothetical.

- Your question is worthy of proper consideration. Perhaps I can just take a moment to consider it before answering.
- I looked at that question and many others and concluded that it did not have any influence on the events, and so I did not pursue it.
- Of course, your expert has my respect. Your expert's report is perfectly understandable but that does not mean I can accept his opinion when in my view it is wrong.

7.6 Cross Examination

Please, please, please, do not make the most fundamental error that undermines experts regularly in cross examination and overstate your CV.

I heard the head of a TV station being questioned on the radio just a couple of years ago. He had declared himself to have been an editor of a UK TV programme called Panorama. When quizzed at first, he stood by his CV, but then the questioner hit him with a killer blow. "But I am the Editor of Panorama". Honestly, you could not make it up could you. But the same thing happened in a case in which I was instructed in Paris.

The opposing delay expert disclosed his CV and had credited himself with the Expert Witness role on one of my cases. He surely knew that I was on the other side of this case. What possessed him? When counsel tested his CV further, he claimed to have been the expert witness on another case relating to a national football stadium, but the lawyers on that particular case were my instructing lawyers in this case and they couldn't remember him being involved. Eventually, the Tribunal had to stop the cross examination of the expert on his wayward CV because it became too embarrassing for all involved. In the award his evidence was not just dismissed it was disregarded and not mentioned at all, and the Tribunal followed my findings.

If I had been that expert's client, I would have wanted my money back. I believe that expert now works abroad.

I have been cross examined on my experience, my published textbooks, and my alleged role as a "professional expert", an expert who does no real work but who opines only. The dialogue usually goes like this:

QC: Mr Whitfield it is true, is it not, that you are a professional expert witness.

Me: If you mean, have I given up my amateur status and am now being paid, then yes, I am a professional.

QC: I have looked at your CV and you carry out only expert assignments, is that not the case?

Me: No.

QC: When was the last time you worked on an ongoing project that was not in dispute.

Me: Last Friday. I left the project where I am assisting with the project management to come to this hearing.

QC: OK, let's move on.

Be bold but try not to joust with the advocate as he is likely to be very adept and experienced at arguing and such repartee does not amuse the tribunal.

Be sure to answer all questions honestly and admit if you do not remember where something is in your report. Counsel may make a snide remark, but it will not influence the tribunal. If you do not know the answer to a question say so, and do not offer to find the answer unless pressed to do so or you will end up with some homework overnight.

In my first court case in London, in what was then the Official Referees Court in Fetter Lane, I was testifying on a case where a project had become a cost-plus contract despite its beginnings as a measure and value contract. The court accepted that it was inevitable that conversion of the lump sum contract to a cost-plus contract would have to be allowed because the contractor's operatives had been conscripted by the client to do its bidding and on its timetable.

During my testimony the opposing counsel hit on a new line of questioning, not a line of enquiry that the experts had concerned themselves with as we had agreed that the hours worked should be paid as documented and signed for. Counsel asked the question, "How does the cost for materials and manpower in the telephone service cabling compare to the value if measured and priced at bill rates?"

"I don't know." I replied. "The experts valued the works as pleaded and defended, on a cost-plus basis. In any event the telephone cabling was an additional scope of works, and so no prices were offered or accepted."

Brilliant. I was pleased with myself. Opposing counsel looked glum but satisfied, and then the Judge looked at me and said, "I too am curious as to the comparison. Could you give an estimate if you were given time?" Obviously, I could. I was a QS after all. How could I refuse?

I left the court with a roll of drawings and a copy of Spon's Electrical & Mechanical Price Book under my arm and spent a night (until 3am) measuring and valuing the telecoms cabling in the Canary Wharf Tower. Given the generous nature of Spon's prices, the measure and value exercise roughly equated to the cost-plus evaluation, and everyone was happy, except me.

Another tip is to always answer questions fully even if it takes a long time. You may see opposing counsel play acting boredom but ignore him. Your answer is for the benefit of the tribunal. If he interrupts and suggests that he has heard enough, explain that unless you complete your answer you are concerned that you may mislead the tribunal and let them decide what to do.

In any hearing room try not to be concerned at anyone else's actions. Frantic activity in the opposition team and paper passing may be alarming to you. "Oh no, what have they found/ what have I said?" you may think but is often just pre-arranged role play.

In most of my recent cases I have been asked to give evidence sitting alongside my opposing expert. Counsel and the Tribunal members will then ask a question of both experts and try to understand why they do not agree. They will even encourage you to discuss matters in front of them. The colloquial term for this is 'hot-tubbing', but no swimwear is required, you just sit side by side and answer questions from all-comers. The process is also known more formally as concurrent evidence.

It is important to note that as well as your expert role in testifying, you may be asked to assist in other areas of the case presentation too.

7.7 Expert Assistance at Trial

If you are the expert for the claimant/plaintiff/prosecution, you will probably give your evidence first. The responding or defending experts usually come close to last. Whichever position in the proceedings is assigned to you, your instructing lawyers will probably want you to listen to the witnesses and help provide cross examination questions relating to your instructions. You will be a team member in that respect. In some cases, this may not be allowed for reasons of fairness.

You may also find that you have a role to play in disclosure of documents or in the assembly of the documents for the hearing. In real life, many and varied are the tasks assigned to experts when things get busy.

I recall an arbitration in Geneva where my hotel was also the arbitration venue. The hearing ran from 9am until 4pm each day and then we took a break. At 9pm we began a series of meetings to prepare witnesses and evidence for the next day. One night I was assisting between 11pm and 1am, the next night 1am to 3am and the third night from 5:30am to 8:30am.

On the upside, it was a five-star hotel overlooking the historic lake.

7.8 Judgements and Awards

These can be a long time in coming, usually months but sometimes longer. When they arrive, you may be mentioned a little, a lot or not at all. Comments may be neutral, positive, or negative. Earlier, we talked about one opposing expert whose career was killed by a single judgement and another who is now practising abroad. Negative judgements and a judge's asides can be devastating to an expert career. Positive comments, however, can make an expert immensely popular.

In my first testifying case I was still 33-year-old Quantity Surveyor, and quite young for an expert witness, but the judge took a shine to me. He asked kindly questions about my young family and made sure I was comfortable before giving evidence. I will never forget his judgement because my first case turned out to be one of the highlights of my career. He wrote of me; "Mr Whitfield is the very model of an expert witness."

So, come on, let us all testify in a way that our mothers would be proud of and we can all be model expert witnesses.

Section 8:

The Better Expert Witness in You

8.1 Introduction

By 1994 I was speaking at industry dinners, CPD days, Internal and External seminars, professional bodies' conferences, and expert witness training days. I was also preparing and presenting 1, 2 and 3-day seminars on negotiation for a well-known international seminar provider. In some instances, I found myself speaking to people way beyond our industry. For example, I once presented a negotiation seminar to a group of salespeople and administrators from the Bovril Factory in Burton on Trent.

All because I chose to specialise. Just like you, I wanted to be an expert in something.

When public speaking, I try to begin with a funny anecdote or joke to settle people in and let them relax. One day I found myself in Texas, USA speaking to a large group of lawyers. I had them for the whole morning. At 8:30am I began with some of my funniest stories. Not a titter, not even so much as a smile. This was going to be a long day, but not as long as the faces in the unforgiving crowd.

At the first break, around 10am, the leader of the group approached me, and I thought that my US speaking career was coming to an end.

"Excuse me, sir," he politely began in a Texas drawl that told you to expect at least one Y'all, in the next sentence or two. "We know that you are a serious guy, but some of those things you were saying were real funny. We didn't want to laugh, what with you being British and all. But would you mind if we just let ourselves go a little?"

I was so relieved. We went on to have a great day.

I am supremely fortunate. Being an expert witness has taken me to 39 countries and has made me friends in many more. There is more to an expert life than simply hard work and dedication, there is a big payoff.

Because of our good fortune we each need to pay it forward, and let others benefit as well.

One day, in the midst of a long hearing in London, my young and talented assistant, Suzanne, celebrated her birthday quietly with a call from home. She spoke to her partner, another of my assistants, and her parents. That was the limit of her expectations from her birthday and her expert foray to the UK from Dubai. Unbeknown to her, I had booked us both dinner at a delightful restaurant, followed by a theatre visit to see a comedic version of the 39 Steps. We spent a wonderful evening together and the next day she sat as expert second chair and helped the legal team as I testified.

It wasn't exactly an Oscars After Party at the Kardashians, but it made our transient life a bit more enjoyable.

Once I began working closely with my new team it didn't take me long to recognise that Suzanne and all of my other colleagues were more than capable of being experts in their own right. How gratifying that is for me, and how valuable that is for the dispute industry. New and young experts need to be given opportunities to thrive and survive in the challenging arena of dispute resolution.

8.2 The Expert in Society

As I noted at the beginning of this textbook, experts are drawn from all professions, trades and pastimes. They also come from every gender, race, creed and religion. They might look like a fashion model or, like me, they might not. They may be able bodied, or they may have overcome great physical, or physiological challenges. In their quiet moments they may be an introvert sock collector or an extrovert instagrammer.

Experts are not a type, nor should they be. If you are reading this, you can be an expert.

There are, however, a number of attributes that you will need to have, or adopt, if you want to be a successful expert witness. I will list and describe some of these attributes. My list is not exclusive, nor do you have to encompass them all, but individually they should all help to make you a 'go to' expert.

8.3 A General Education

It is fantastic that we have specialist courses at universities and other bodies of learning, courses that did not exist just twenty years ago. Focussed learning, such as that in master's courses, is essential for someone who wants to specialise as an expert, but a wider education helps too.

Alongside our own profession, a basic knowledge or understanding of the law is probably an imperative for testifying experts. Not because we want to cite case law and depend on precedent in our reports - we certainly do not - but because we need to understand the importance of legal developments. Sometimes, that knowledge, that we thought long forgotten, can come to the forefronts of our minds just when it is needed.

I recall being in a Kuwait restaurant brainstorming a case with a Law Partner and a younger assistant, after a bruising meeting with the opposition. We all felt that the justice of the case lay with our client, who was being railroaded by a much larger opponent. We had a decent case but there existed documentation that could heavily influence valuation. It was in our client's interests that the document be seen and considered by the Tribunal. The opposition had presented a reasonable argument for its exclusion, even though their client had originally introduced the document.

We talked for a while and then my mind flicked back to a law tutorial in London many years before. Estoppel came to mind, and I said it out loud. Both lawyers became animated and we hurried our remaining courses so that they could get back to the hotel and see if estoppel could help us. It did. Our brilliant legal team prevented the opposition from denying our client the right to rely on a document that they had issued, and our client had acted upon.

On another occasion I was working with a young fellow delay analyst who loved gaming and computing. When a complex project became almost too complex for our delay expert to explain to the Tribunal in narrative form, he stepped in and created a computer model in the form of a game. The Tribunal could click on a graphic and that section of the works would appear on the screen in graphic form, in three colourful dimensions. Suddenly the conflicts and clashes were obvious to the Tribunal and our delay expert's argument was supported.

I like photography and know some great photographers, so when a problem arose on one of my expert appointments relating to record photographs that my client insisted were incorrectly dated, I called on a friend. She pointed out that if we could get the raw file, she could interrogate it with her photo software. She was able to show that the EXIF information attached to the photo indicated that the photos were taken before the date alleged, thus discrediting the consultant's argument justifying non-payment of a certificate. If you want to try this for yourself simply right click on the original photo file, open properties and go to the details folder. You will see when it was taken, the time, whether flash was used and many more interesting things. My camera even has geo plotting and so we can see exactly where a photo was taken.

So, as previously explained, a general understanding of other areas of expertise, along with a good general education will help you as an expert, both when socialising and when reporting.

I have also mentioned in these pages that I studied psychology for a semester at college. In another semester I studied music appreciation. Some things help your career, some just help you retain your sanity when under pressure.

I recommend that you read or listen to self-help guides and broaden your interests. General intellectual ability is impressive to others, and more impressive than you might think. My wife and I have travelled around the UK and the USA listening to books on philosophy, space, quantum mechanics and the human brain. It helps us converse widely and enables us to show interest in others who have similar interests, a key behaviour in establishing rapport.

I was in a hearing a couple of years ago when the lawyer, an American, said, "Our case is a little unsteady. We need you to go in there and use that professorial voice you adopt and tell them how it is". I had never realised that I sounded authoritarian. I have always cultivated exactly the opposite approach, to no avail obviously. But somehow, I had persuaded my lawyers that I was learned when I am little more than well informed.

Intelligent, coherent, well-read experts who are comfortable with their expertise and who are generally interesting will not only be hired, they will be convincing in their testimony.

8.4 Determination and Patience

Thomas Fuller, English Theologian, once said that the darkest hour is just before dawn. Sadly, it is not factually true (apologies also to the *Mamas and Papas* who had a hit song with the same premise), but it is allegorically useful. Experts who are determined and persistent will often find that an answer appears just when they are despairing because it appears that no solution is available.

Film Studio mogul, Samuel Goldwyn is credited with first saying, 'The harder I work, the luckier I get.' Anyone who has fulfilled a marketing role will understand this sentiment. He also said,

"I think luck is the sense to recognize an opportunity and the ability to take advantage of it. The man who can smile at his breaks and grab his chances gets on." Experts might do well to have this saying on the wall over their desk.

In my experience, the best experts have a grim determination to find the right answer. The worst experts find an answer, any answer, and stop looking. It takes time to become the expert you aspire to be. Be patient but never lose the determination. I for one am often humbled by the dedication of others.

In an early case, around 1993, myself and the instructing lawyer were due to travel to London to meet with counsel in Essex Street. I offered to accompany him on the train. He assured me he would be fine making his own way and would meet me at Temple Tube Station at the entrance overlooking the gardens. I was worried for him because my instructing solicitor was entirely blind and had only a white stick for guidance. Nonetheless, he was there waiting for me when I arrived.

I was impressed as we traversed London for the rest of the day, with him leading much of the time and interlocking his arm with mine only when he was in unfamiliar territory. He had determinedly counted the tube steps for the stations he commonly used. He knew where the entrance to chambers was by counting steps. He felt the railings and knew he had arrived. He pointed out that the flowers in the hanging baskets always gave away the location in the spring and the summer.

That was commitment of the highest calibre. He could have stayed in Tyneside and called in by phone, but he wanted to be in the same room as the barrister, as we discussed the case.

Inspired by his example, when I was on holiday in South Africa, I was determined to master jet skiing. I made my first attempts on a primitive machine, one where you started lying down, rose to your knees and eventually stood, as there was no seat. To make matters worse, the jet ski did not stand naturally upright in the water, it only became upright when moving quickly through the water. Anyway, I took my instructions and set off.

It all began well enough. I lay flat and turned the throttle, then as the jet ski moved, I was readying myself to move to a kneeling position and then a standing position. Therein lay the problem. As the jet ski took off, the twin jets powered lake water into my legs, a little uncomfortable but no real problem there. However, as the acceleration almost yanked my arms from their sockets, my body slid backwards. The powerful jets which had been blasting my legs with only minor discomfort, were now firing jets of water at point blank range into my groin. Now that real discomfort quickly escalated into teeth clenching pain. To maintain my ambition to have more children, I let go and had to swim after the jet ski which was now circling on its side. I started again and the same happened again. I had almost circled the entire lake in comedic, and painful, acrobatics by the time I got my knees to where they should have been.

Meanwhile, on the beach, an interested crowd had gathered to see how long it would take the pasty skinned Englishman to drown. At the front of the crowd were my sister and father.

"He will give up when he gets back to the beach," my father announced.

"No, he won't," my sister argued, "He is stubborn, and he paid for thirty minutes!"

I believe the word she was looking for was 'persistent'. I eventually stood up and circled the lake a few times before coming in at the end of my rental time to a mixture of laughter and applause. I had conquered the jet ski, the lake, and by extrapolation, the entire continent of Africa.

8.5 Qualifications and Experience

Qualifications are a means by which others can know your level of learning. Anyone who has completed a degree will admit (albeit secretly to themselves) that this is a poor tool of choice for such an important selection.

Nonetheless, qualifications, and memberships of organisations who have challenging standards of entry, are paramount in the minds of those appointing experts. The other thing people will look for is experience.

When I qualified, I was expected to keep an 'experience diary' for two years to gain chartered status. Unfortunately for me, the panel at the RICS at the time considered my experience with a contractor to be somehow inferior to private practice. I disagreed. I was commercial director responsible for making profits of a million pounds a year, but they would not budge.

I wanted my Chartered status, and so I agreed with my employer that I would work three days a week at my normal job and two days a week gaining other experience, during the summer months.

I spent my time working for a top QS practice one day a week, settling M&E Final Accounts, because they did not have an M&E QS, and one day a week at a loss adjusting practice on the floor above ours in the office building.

I learned a lot that summer and was granted my parchment in the autumn. In later years, my brief experience in loss adjusting won me a valuable assignment as expert on a major oil rig Insurance claim. Prior to that I was approached by a Swiss Controls company to be Commercial Manager for the UK and USA. They only knew me because I had settled their final accounts on my one day a week in private practice. I spent a happy couple of years flying the world with them, thanks to what was little more than a stroke of luck.

All in all, the elderly panel at the RICS did me a favour.

I have since learned to never turn down the opportunity to gain experience, to try something new or to learn a new skill. I believe that it was Darwin who said that the species with the widest range of behaviours would be the most likely to survive. I agree with Darwin on this point. I believe that the expert with the widest range of genuine skills will be busiest.

8.6 Personality

I believe that many different personality types can successfully practice as experts, but all will face challenges.

	People Oriented	Task Oriented	
Assertive	Entertainer	RULER	Aggressive
Passive	Admirer	Analytic	Submissive

We should all try to establish where we lie in my crude personality matrix above. Doing so will help us negotiate our future expert relationships. I have found that a lot of successful experts sit above the assertiveness line, and the best experts usually tend towards the People oriented side of the chart.

All experts will discover that they have, and need, behaviours that belong in each quadrant. However, the best experts will not be submissive or passive, they will be assertive without being aggressive. Many will be entertainers with a grounding in the analytic quadrant.

It is important to recognise that personalities are made, not imposed; we can train ourselves to be confident public speakers, for example, but no matter our success we must never lose our humility. We need to remember our beginnings, our training, our education. We must accept that from our parents, teachers, friends, colleagues and others we have been given life, and a reason for living it. The expert I would want to instruct is self-aware without being self-aggrandised, is independent whilst recognising that co-dependence is necessary in real life. I would want to instruct an expert who cares about me and my case. I do not want a remote and cold expert, I want one who melds evidence, empathy and fairness seamlessly into their opinion.

Maybe you have different views, and so you should. We all need to be the expert we feel comfortable with being. If you currently feel unsettled about your personal standing in the expert community, perhaps now is a good time to review your situation. If it's not enjoyable, you may be doing it wrong.

8.7 Goat Yoga, Wokeness and the Expert

Just recently Goat Yoga has become something of a phenomenon in the UK. Many providers have used American or African Pygmy Goats, but others have used baby goats. The problem is that baby goats grow into adult goats, which are then of no use in goat yoga. Thus, they are sold, often for meat, and meet an untimely death. Not the outcome a caring yoga enthusiast would expect from an exercise in mindfulness. This was just one more fashionable offering that was not thought through properly. As experts we cannot afford to fall into the trap of following fashions blindly.

I understand that in every generation there are trends and fashions. When I started work my hair reached my shoulders. Perhaps unwisely, I wore platform shoes and Ben Sherman shirts with narrow woven ties. I once had a droopy moustache. Eventually, trends pass, fashions fade and only the substantive remains.

As an upcoming expert witness, you must be wary of new trends and fashions in the construction disputes industry. Over the years the disputes industry has adopted many new fashionable ideas and has dropped almost as many. For example, try and find anyone who actively supports the use of the Hudson Formula or Emden's Formula, once so beloved of claims consultants around the world.

The last time I came across this formulaic approach was in 2016 when a contractor calculated a Head Office Overhead contribution of US$32,000.00 per day, using Hudson's Formula. I calculated the actual head office cost contribution at less than 10% of that figure, using real evidence from their own records.

If you want another example of how trends quickly become outdated, you could take a look at the SCL Protocol first and second editions. In the context of the section on delay analysis methodology, the advice has changed considerably in just a few years.

The secret to substantive expert witness success is in remembering why we are there and what we are doing. We are not there to exhibit our own cleverness, nor should we advocate a new trendy approach to a Tribunal unless it is provably better than the existing approach.

Another trend we see in the world today is given the name *Wokeness*. In my view *Wokeness* is a fine attribute; we used to call it awareness. But, call it what you might, the best experts will need to be aware of societal and construction industry change and embrace it. Experts need to be current, up to date. There are more new exciting innovations in expert work just around the corner. I know it. I have considerable faith in the next generation of experts to innovate and simplify. To be a great expert you need to be ready to embrace change, if it proves to be beneficial.

Overall, my advice is this; when a new trend is being proposed, do your due diligence before rushing headlong into acceptance. You are an expert instructed to give opinion based on your sound experience, not on an untried technology or theory proposed by others.

8.8 The Better Expert in You

I guess that I am in the autumn of my expert years and, as I look at my opponents and colleagues today, I see the promise of better experts tomorrow.

Continued education and learning are pre-requisites for young people now, and an understanding of technology is demanded. Young experts are facing ever more complex construction projects as towers go higher, stadia bigger and transport links go further.

This is probably a new golden age for construction experts. The older experts need to mentor and champion the next generation, while clients must give opportunities to those who are able but who have not yet testified.

Despite comments to the contrary, in my experience tribunals and courts have always been accepting of new but skilled, professionally qualified and enthusiastic witnesses. Instructing solicitors and their clients now need to look to the future and give new experts real opportunities to testify.

By reading this book of anecdotal nonsense, and good sound expert advice, along with many other more learned texts, you are signalling to the world that you want to improve your expert skills.

As you improve your skills you improve your capability and, ultimately, your expert witness ranking.

I appreciate that this book is something of an irreverent foray into the world of expert witness work, but that is my modus operandi, I do not think I will change now.

Nonetheless, for all of its lightness and ephemera, this book contains truths. Truths that have been learned over many years; truths I have been taught by others much brighter than me. Take what you can from others and build on it. There is no better way to see farther than to stand on the shoulder of giants. It worked for me, and I hope it works for you.

Be true to yourself, stay grounded, and you will become the best expert you can be.

Printed in Great Britain
by Amazon

41029778R00056